LOVE THAT STORY

LOVE THAT STORY

Observations from a Gorgeously Queer Life

JONATHAN VAN NESS

HarperOne
An Imprint of HarperCollinsPublishers

Some names have been changed to protect people's privacy.

HarperCollins books may be purchased for educational, business, or sales pro-
motional use. For information, please email the Special Markets Department at
SPsales@harpercollins.com.

FIRST EDITION

Designed by Yvonne Chan

Library of Congress Cataloging-in-Publication Data has been applied for.

ISBN 978-0-06-308226-7

22 23 24 25 26 LSC 10 9 8 7 6 5 4 3 2 1

To those who choose

curiosity and compassion,

loving themselves,

and asking for help

should they ever lose their way

CONTENTS

LOVE THAT STORY

NOW, WHERE WERE WE?

My thirty-first trip around the sun brought on opportunities I had always dreamed of. I wrote a *New York Times* bestselling memoir, I sold out Radio City Music Hall on my first headlining stand-up comedy tour, and I was nominated for my second Emmy. I even got to realize my lifelong dream of learning to figure skate.

It all seemed surreal, especially because in the years leading up to that thirty-first trip around the sun, I'd taken a very early detour onto Trauma Boulevard, and later made a few pit stops on Sexual Compulsivity Lane and Hardcore Drug Use Road, before finally exiting on the healing journey off-ramp I'm still on to this day. Sometimes my route feels more chaotic than Michelle Kwan's win at the 2000 World Figure Skating Championships, where she came back from third place to clinch her third World title. All to say, not everything works out the way we think it will, but that doesn't mean that our experience is anything less than valid.

Only in hindsight can I see that I achieved my dreams because of, not in spite of, all the bumps in the road. I had to go through everything I did to get to where I am. I'm still learning and growing, but honestly, there's nothing about my life I would change.

I find that my mind wants to categorize events past and present and put them into tidy little mental boxes. I think it's my brain trying to have a functional understanding so I can process that topic or experience, check it off on my list, and say, "I get it." But I'm constantly trying to deepen my understanding of the world and acknowledge that good and bad can coexist and that we will never be able to just snap our fingers and put everything in its place. While a part of me has always been focused on getting somewhere "better," I am always simultaneously looking for ways to try to engage and stay curious and connected about where I am in the process. To quote Kacey Musgraves, I have been "happy and sad at the same time," and life just be like that sometimes.

This felt especially true while writing my first book.

In that process, I learned that writing a memoir is like figure skating: it looks effortless and beautiful from the outside, while in reality, you stretch thy groin so much that you nearly split yourself in half for the whole world to see. But in the iconic words of Whoopi Goldberg in *Sister Act 2*, "If you wake up in the mornin' and you can't think of anything but singin' first, then you're supposed to be a singer, girl." I can't sing, but every morning I woke up feeling inspired to express myself on the page and on the ice. Luckily, I was able to learn to do both and I became a bestselling author. As for an Olympic figure skater, I'm still an Olympic-level figure skating . . . fan.

I knew I was in for a rough journey when I first decided to tell my story in *Over the Top*. Aside from figuring out the mental discipline required to actually sit myself down every single day and do the writing (a process that consisted of consuming countless cups of coffee, cannabis, and cinnamon streusel cakes from Trader Joe's before I could really hit my groove), I knew that in order to tell my truth accurately I'd need to relive the most intense and hurtful moments I've ever experienced. If you haven't written a memoir yourself, just imagine going to therapy to discuss your deepest trauma every single morning for a year, only there's no actual therapist there to help you process what you're sharing about yourself. (I do have an amazing therapist, thank God, but with my sessions only happening once or twice a week, it felt like swallowing a couple of Advil after being run over daily by a Mack truck.)

Coming out very publicly about my HIV+ status, surviving sexual abuse, and overcoming hardcore drug use was a healing yet harrowing experience. Luckily, I also had many joyful memories to write about. I hoped sharing my story would help other people going through similar hardships, and that helped balance out the nerve-racking and painful parts. Still, by the time the final draft was completed and on its way to the printer, all I could think was: *That was like wearing the skinniest stiletto heels ever, but I just got home and now I can take them off—the hard part is over.*

Don't get me wrong. The book was something I hadn't even dared dream was possible, and I'm still overwhelmed with gratitude that my publisher and editor believed in me and felt that I had a story worth telling. However, after over a year of diligently laboring in love, writing my story the way I wanted it to be told, hoping it would inspire people or help them in their healing journey, I was ready to move forward. Once the book came out, I learned quickly that it's hard to move forward when you're constantly being dragged back into the past: promoting it meant reliving the darker moments of my life all over again. And again. And again.

Each time I did another interview, I was pulled right back into everything I'd gone through, always in front of a different stranger, and every one of them with their own agenda and a series of probing questions about times in my life that I thought I'd made peace with. As more and more of these interviews piled up, I began to wonder if I actually had.

I also didn't anticipate how readers still coming to terms with their HIV status would suddenly see me as a source of strength. This was humbling but also added whole new layers of pressure and doubt. Could I really be that person for them? Answering questions from people I'd never met, helping them find doctors, and not quite knowing how the HIV safety net worked in whatever state, or sometimes country, they were in often made me feel useless about the best way to guide them.

And that wasn't all. Survivors who were still processing their own sexual abuse now viewed me as a confidant with whom they could share their stories. It gave me a whole new level of empathy, and I can't overstate how honored I am whenever someone feels safe enough with me to discuss their pain. But sometimes having an incredibly intense and intimate conversation and taking on that energy made it hard to turn on a dime when I had to interact with someone from the press immediately afterwards and suddenly become my giggly, happy JVN self.

I'm not trying to complain or be an ungrateful nightmare. I just thought writing the book would be the most challenging part, but that was shortsighted of me, because for folks who read my story and found that it resonated with them, obviously the book coming out would only be the beginning. And for those who read or heard about my book who don't relate to me, well, hey, call me an optimist, but I definitely didn't expect all the rage-inducing transphobic, homophobic, HIV-stigmatizing ignorance that has been hurled my way. And one of the hardest parts was at the very beginning.

Over the Top came out on September 24, 2019, and in the weeks leading up to my publication date I was a nervous wreck. That's pretty normal for any debut author, and luckily I had a ton of work on my plate to distract me. I was in the middle of my first international comedy tour (much more about that later) and had the Creative Arts Emmys to look forward to. *Queer Eye* had been nominated for six of them, and the cast and crew were excitedly preparing for the ceremony. I even had a nomination of my own for *Gay of Thrones*, for Outstanding Short Form Variety Series.

About a month before the book's release, I landed my first big sit-down interview about it with a reporter from an important newspaper. He'd scheduled a breakfast date at a little corner café just a few blocks from my apartment in New York City, and walking there that morning I felt just like Carrie Bradshaw in the opening credits of *Sex and the City*, except with heartburn and a deep fear that I was about to diarrhea my tutu all over the sidewalk.

This would be the first time I'd spoken about the book to anyone outside my immediate circle of friends and family, and I was dying to know what the journalist thought of the project I'd poured so much of myself into.

I arrived at the café, introduced myself to the writer, and

soon after we were seated, he asked, "True or false: your book covers disordered eating."

I felt stunned. Sure, I'd written some epic descriptions of the multitudes of sugary snacks I basically lived on for the first, well, all of the years of my life, but *that* was his take-away? That I had an eating disorder? Doesn't everyone fantasize about Double Decker tacos being added back to Taco Bell's menu? I'd included those details in the book because I thought they were funny. Suddenly, they felt like a worrisome addition.

"Well, I hadn't really thought of it like that," I answered slowly, "but I guess I can see how it seems that way."

I was still trying to unpack his interpretation of those scenes in the book as he proceeded with more questions, many of them having to do with my coming out as HIV+. We treated it like a casual conversation—casual if that means discussing my most intimate life moments with a total stranger in a restaurant, seated in close proximity to a crowd of more strangers, all of whom were tilting their ears towards our booth.

Have you ever had that classic anxiety nightmare about arriving at school, realizing you're naked, and everyone is looking at you and whispering? That's what becoming famous feels like. It's a lot of attention whether you're ready for it or not—on the street, in a bar, at a party, sometimes even in a public bathroom. I wasn't quite used to it yet. (I'm still not, tbh.)

Right in the middle of detailing the exact moment I discovered I was HIV+, two very sweet, well-intentioned girls appeared at our table and asked if they could take a selfie. It's a situation I'm used to because it happens all the time. Usually I happily oblige, but in this instance, I literally had tears in my eyes. Even if they hadn't heard the specifics of what I'd been saying, this was clearly not the right time.

But at that moment my obvious distress didn't matter. They wanted their photo, and I just couldn't do it. There was no way I could flip a switch and turn on the happy JVN they knew from TV. I apologized and explained that I was having a very intense conversation, said, "Namaste," and went back to talking about HIV, surviving sexual abuse, and becoming a sex worker. Just your average brunch moment, right?

By the time the interview was over I felt utterly emotionally drained, and also very worried. I'd just spilled so much information I'd kept secret for so long. I was prepared to do that with the book, but what comforted me about going public about my past was the fact that I'd been given a chance to tell my stories in my own words. Suddenly I was no longer sure that would be the case, so I called my publicist to confirm that the interview would come out after my book had been released.

"Well," she told me, "they don't reveal the exact date that they're going to publish their articles. But it will be before the book hits the shelves, anywhere from two to four days. That's normal—it's all part of the process."

I suddenly worried for the second time that day that anxiety shit was about to start running down my legs. This was all new territory for me. I was shocked and wished I'd known the timing of it all before I'd sat down with the reporter.

I get it now. Books need publicity ahead of their publishing date. My publicist was right, it's a normal part of the process and one I was very lucky to be a part of, but in that moment all I could think was: *Oh my fuck, oh my Nancy Kerrigan, holy Simone Biles—what am I going to do?*

I began to obsess over how the article would be written and how it would be received. I still had my comedy tour to get back to, and the red carpet to prepare for, but now I woke up with dread every morning. Stepping onto the stage for each nightly stand-up show introduced a whole new element of risk; before that first book interview, my pre-performance nerves had always been about whether the audience would laugh at my jokes or if I'd land the difficult-for-me gymnastics routine I did at the beginning of each show (as any nonbinary, gymnastics-obsessed, newbie, traveling stand-up comedian does in their act). But during the following few weeks of shows, I worried constantly in the back of my mind that while I was on stage, my most private moments were being released into the world and racing across the internet like Bonnie Blair on her way to speed skating glory, flinging my secrets everywhere like ice shavings in her wake, without any of the care I'd given my words in the book.

I tried hard to put the impending article out of my mind. I had more shows to slay and people to dazzle with my comedy prowess, but the worries lingered.

Three days before my publication date, I returned home to New York after a show in Las Vegas, prior to which I had been in Toronto doing stand-up and, before that, with the cast and crew of *Queer Eye* at the Creative Arts Emmys in LA. At each event I wondered if I'd be on the red carpet or mid-interview when all of a sudden everyone would know my HIV status and personal struggles, but told through someone else's narrative. I passed out as soon as I got home that Saturday night and woke up around eleven on Sunday with dozens of texts and even more missed calls.

Clearly, the article had gone live.

Reading the story on the couch in my living room, curled up next to my best friend, surrounded by the luggage we'd tossed on the floor just hours before, was a sobering experience. The journalist had written an authentic, candid, and fair article, and to my relief, the overall reactions throughout the day were very positive. But my interaction with the two girls asking for a picture became a big focus of the story. As had every deep, dark, clickbait fact about my past.

If I hadn't known otherwise, my book kind of sounded like a downer.

Where's all the fun stuff? I wondered. *The lightness? The laughter? All of my brilliant, encyclopedic Michelle Kwan references?* I wasn't ashamed of the facts I'd laid bare, but that wasn't the totality of my story. So much of it is about learning that some of my biggest successes live next to some of my biggest traumas, and that's okay. I wanted to show people that joy can live beside sorrow, and that sadness doesn't invalidate your right to experience happiness. The book is about how I learned to love myself despite all the reasons I could have chosen not to, and I wanted other people to discover the same ability in themselves. Instead, the world's first impression of my book, warts and all, highlighted all of the warts and none of the all.

A lasting effect of that article was that it also set the tone for more to follow. Many of the healing stories in my book were neglected, and subsequent reporters kept the emphasis firmly on the darkness. Finding the courage to tell my truth and then having it retold in what felt like a more negative light felt frustrating.

I understand now that their priority wasn't my personal feelings or the overall message; it was boosting their readership. And while it took me a hot second to come around to this, that's ultimately okay because their mission ended up also serving mine. It introduced me to a wider audience than I'd dared to hope for. The book became a bestseller, and my dream that it would help people came true.

I'm grateful, because in the end, the experience taught me whole new levels of compassion, patience, and, most important, acceptance. In fact, I learned to thrive despite the discomfort of every new interview with a person who had only skimmed the book and then came at me with a preconceived notion of who I am. I realized that each of those situations were moments I could inspire a person to not judge a book by its cover. Or, more specifically, a nonbinary multi-hyphenate by their trauma. Sitting next to James Corden and Allison Janney on *The Late Late Show* and segueing from a fun little game about the history of trains to a story about living with HIV would have given most people watching late-night television whiplash, but by the end of my tour, these discussions came much more naturally, and I felt like I had begun to redefine what someone living with HIV looks like.

Despite everything I had to go through to tell my story, the response from the readers themselves validated why I wrote the book in the first place. The support was overwhelming, and hearing from people who found comfort in what I had shared was not only reassuring, it also answered the deeper and more personal question I had posed in the book: If people learned everything there was to know about me, would they still love me?

I experienced a resounding *yes* from so many readers who recognized aspects of themselves in my story, and that's comforting beyond words. Seeing ourselves in someone else's vulnerability makes us all feel less alone. The fear of being unlovable due to past experiences is the literal definition of shame, and shame isn't something to keep buried. It needs to be brought to the surface, turned around, examined, and processed. It's incredibly difficult work, but it's impossible to live healthy lives as individuals, much less as a society, unless we do it.

And before anyone even tries to start that journey, we must first get comfortable with being uncomfortable.

I'm sure this isn't the first time you've heard that phrase. It's certainly been on my mind for a long time now, especially while doing hundreds of interviews on my weekly podcast *Getting Curious*. Since its start back in 2015, I've been talking to experts about subjects I'm curious about, from the Holocaust to animal communication to the gender binary. I've interviewed Oscar, Emmy, Tony, and Grammy winners, academics, elected officials, historians, journalists, scientists, authors, and more. I've learned so much, and by confronting these sometimes difficult, always complicated topics, I've also been able to feel more at ease when a sticky situation arises in my life. Those uncomfortable moments have inspired a lot of personal growth, and I want to share those moments—and hopefully make people laugh a little along the way. Because we can learn to listen to and absorb things that are uncomfortable yet so necessary to talk about, like systemic racism or transphobia, while simultaneously learning to love ourselves and one another. Otherwise, we risk turning into a country completely made up of Marjorie Taylor Greenes.

I decided to write this book of essays to share some of what I've observed through the years and because I'm curious about different ways I can continue to grow and be a better person. If you're holding this book in your hands, I bet you feel the same. You're not going to find quickie here's-how-to-heal-yourself-in-ten-steps lists here. The kind of internal/external work that we all need to do is an ongoing process. There are no simple answers to any of the subjects I write about here. My own internalized shame still runs deep, despite all the work I've done—and still do—to try and heal it. The bubbly and happy JVN you see on *Queer Eye* is a strong and vital part of my authentic self, but I still get weighed down by doubt and insecurity just like anyone else. We're all human, but somewhere in the timeline of history we lost a part of our humanity. Vulnerability became something to hide from the world, viewed as weakness, when in fact embracing that part of ourselves is one of the most necessary tools in our mental arsenal to help us evolve, and thrive.

In this essay collection, I'm continuing to challenge my internalized shame wherever I find it rearing its ugly head—a multitude of situations that include trying to figure out if it's appropriate to express earth-shattering grief at work, feeling comfortable in dresses and heels, working to improve the HIV safety net, and addressing my own family's complicity in America's systemic racism.

My hope for this book is that I can learn to process the noise of my experiences, find better ways to handle all of it, and share it with you along the way. I want to become so compassionate and educated that I could listen to a full-on QAnon supporter, a rabid Republican, or even just someone who believes that a three-in-one shampoo, conditioner, and body wash is perfectly acceptable, and be able to sit with them, hold space for them, convince them otherwise, all while not ripping my last thirty-seven hairline hairs out in the fucking process.

I've also researched topics I'm curious about to try and answer some of the questions I find myself constantly mulling, like: How did we get to this point—the criminalization and vilification of marijuana; loathing our own beautiful bodies; and hatred against the LGBTQIA+ community? People love to say "Stay in your lane" to celebrities. Well, I say, *"Fuck that."* I've been a queer gender-nonconforming person living with HIV for longer than I've been a celebrity, and even if that wasn't the case, the health and well-being of the people in our country affects my nervous system. I don't want people to suffer, and I will educate myself and share what I learn to hopefully move us a little closer to ending any suffering that I can.

And luckily, this time around, I understand what to expect from the whirlwind of opinions, criticisms, validations, emotions, and anxiety that comes with putting my vulnerabilities into a book. How my stories are received isn't the point. The darkness I've survived doesn't define me. But it is central to who I am, and it allows me to sit with conversations and situations that feel a bit uncomfy. When you've stared down addiction, abuse, and trauma, you get bored with small talk. Give me authenticity. I want to keep learning, keep writing, and keep sharing with you as we do a whirlwind tour of topics that invite us to examine assumptions, expand horizons, and learn more about what makes us all so messy and gorgeous.

CHAPTER 1

PROCESSING GRIEF

Or, ew, did you just make fun of me after my cat died?

Before I landed *Queer Eye*, when I was still building up my hair clientele in Los Angeles, Yelp reviews were critical to your success. I kept a laser eye on them because I'd heard so many horror stories about how a single bad review—whether it was a true experience or not—could negatively impact one's business. Some salon owners were plagued by nasty comments, and those public takedowns could ruin reputations or at the very least set a career back several steps.

Luckily, no one ever came for me with a scathing critique, but as I continued to compulsively check Yelp, all of the constant worrying created a different problem. It didn't matter how many glowing five-star reviews I got. Instead, I grew focused on my hunt for mean ones, waiting for the day when someone who'd told me to my face that they loved their gorgeous new fringe went online and told the world I'd butchered their hair and they were now terrified to leave the house.

After I became a public figure, I transferred that same unhealthy behavior to Twitter, which is basically just Yelp for humans. And on Twitter, reviews of me as a person can get pretty brutal.

The majority of comments are very sweet. I get very nice compliments about moments from the show, including appreciation for my choice of crop tops and respect for my ability to break down the plots of *Sister Act 1* and *2* in twenty-eight seconds. But those aren't the ones that stay with me. It's the especially cruel ones that do. I joke around that I'm addicted to doing this, but that's not quite right. It's like my search for mean-spirited words directed at me has become my new compulsive form of masochism. I know it isn't healthy, but positive comments just don't trigger my survival instinct the way negative ones can. Thoughts like *Is this the tweet that will end my career?* are much stickier in my mind than a tweet that reads, "You give me so much hope and confidence!"

God damn it, brain!

Why does my negativity bias have the strength of an elite gymnast? I suppose it's because I trained it just as hard as one with all my old Yelp hunting back in the day.

My therapist says this comes from a part of our reptilian brain that's constantly scanning the horizon for a tiger or a snake to come kill us. A fuzzy bunny isn't going to devour you, but a king cobra can be lethal. (The bunny here being a complimentary tweet and the cobra being a takedown or a criticism.) In other words, what helped our ancestors not get eaten by predators is what has us up at 2 a.m. scrolling through some toxic shit a stranger has said about us to a bunch of other strangers. We're wired for it.

Sometimes Twitter goes up in flames over something I said or wrote, which comes with the territory of speaking your truth. But other times I'll come across generally mean musings about how I looked or acted on certain episodes of *Queer Eye*. I noticed a lot more of those popping up during our fifth season—comments about how I seemed distracted, not there, glassy-eyed. A few people even questioned my mental well-being.

You know what, though? The ones who questioned my mental state were actually pretty astute, because the truth is I wasn't doing so great. In fact, for a while there during filming, I was trying my best to compartmentalize some of the most soul-crushing grief I have ever felt in my life after my cat fell out of my building's window and died.

FILMING *QUEER EYE* is an incredible opportunity to delve into someone else's life, and in every episode, I give myself over to each hero and help in any way I can. I love my job, and I also love that the show allows me to be a hairdresser, a comedian, and an overall entertainer. But as I've spent more time in these different careers, I've realized that I can't stop and take a moment for my personal life, even if I'm going through something incredibly hard. When I signed on to *Queer Eye* I became a beacon of positivity and love, and there are a lot of times when I have to maintain that strength even when I should probably be taking a little time to focus that positivity inward, to let myself mourn when a tragedy happens, like what happened to Bug the Second.

If you haven't read *Over the Top*, I should fill you in on Bug the First. He was a kitten I found when I was eighteen, and he changed my life. For the following thirteen years, that little black cat was my constant companion. He taught me that I could take care of something other than myself (which was quite a work in progress to begin with). Bug gave me a reason to get out of bed during the times when I didn't feel like getting up in the first place.

I lost Bug to kidney failure while we were simultaneously shooting the third and fourth seasons of *Queer Eye*, and his death carved a pit of grief into my stomach that I wasn't prepared for. The first and second season had recently debuted, and there's no road map for becoming highly visible to the public in the space of a few months. (If you have one, let me know.) The devastation, mixed with sudden notoriety and needing to be on and focused, felt like a queer, less-intense version of Mariah Carey navigating the world in the direct aftermath of *Glitter.*

That was when I developed what I call the *Charlotte's Web* rule. In the classic children's book, when Charlotte the spider dies, three of her babies stay with Wilbur the pig to comfort him. I took my cue from this plotline and decided *When one cat dies, I will adopt two* to help heal the sadness. It's much harder to miss your dead cat when you have two kittens running around, right? *(Right??)* So I went to an animal shelter and adopted a black kitty I named Bug the Second and another adorable little gray baby named Liza Meownelli.

I know what you're thinking. You went and adopted another all-black cat and named him the same thing as the one who just died? *Weird.* It's an admittedly specific approach to mourning, but it's one I learned from my grandparents.

Throughout my childhood, they had a cute black teacup poodle named JP, which stood for Just Perfect. Naturally. When one JP would pass on, literally the next day they would adopt another black teacup poodle and give it the same name.

I always thought their mourning was peculiar. Until Bug died. Suddenly in the aftermath of experiencing such a profound loss, one where I couldn't fathom living my life without a sweet little black shadow as my constant companion, it all made sense.

I introduced my two new baby kittens to my surviving cat,

Harry Larry, and the four of us were ready to take on the world. Until I discovered that poor Liza had a horrible case of kitten inflammatory bowel syndrome. It took six months to figure out a diet that wouldn't give her explosive diarrhea—once, literally on my chest when we were snuggling before bed. Since she required so much extra care, Liza went to live with my mom until I was done filming so she could get the full attention required to get a healthy diet figured out, with a plan to integrate her fully and harmoniously back into our family once I was done. With Liza safely at my mom's, I headed off to Philadelphia with Larry and Bug the Second to film season 5 of *Queer Eye*.

This was such an exciting and dynamic time in my life. I loved being back on set, getting to meet our incredible heroes, spending lots of time with my castmates, all while exploring a beautiful new city I'd never gotten to know before. Most days I worked on the show, and any time off was spent spilling my heart into the final edits of my first book, recording the audiobook version, doing research for my podcast, and perfecting the gorgeous gymnastics routine I'd began incorporating into my stand-up shows to keep audiences—and myself—on our toes.

One night, after an exhausting but empowering gymnastics training session, I returned to my temporary apartment on the twelfth floor of a corporate housing high-rise and ordered dinner. As I finished eating, I called one of my best friends, a makeup artist named Patty, for a FaceTime catch-up.

While we were talking, this intense sadness washed over me for no reason at all, and I started to cry. Not a cute little tear rolling down my cheek but a huge let-it-all-out bawling session. I think I'd been working so hard on so much, and for whatever reason, maybe just seeing a loved one's face, it all came pouring out right then in a much-needed emotional release. She started to cry too, but as quickly as the sobs had come, we both began to cackle. I couldn't explain it, but I felt so relieved and happy. There's nothing better than a good cathartic ugly cry with a bestie who will see you through it and then afterwards not give any impression that the out-of-nowhere sob fest was at all unusual or unhinged. Gotta love a good friend.

As we were wrapping up the call my thermostat began to beep, alerting me that the air-conditioning units were no longer working.

Fuck, I thought. *An August night at 100 degrees with no AC? Just my luck.*

The apartment had two big windows, one in the living room and one in the bedroom, but for safety reasons they only opened outward about three or four inches, creating little cheese-wedge openings that did little to help the stifling heat that had already started to creep in. I turned on the ceiling fan above my bed and flopped on top of the covers, hoping I'd let enough air in to fall asleep. After some tossing and turning, I finally did, and woke up early the next morning. I called Patty again to have a good lol about the previous night's random tears, and as we were laughing, I stroked little Larry and called out for Bug the Second, who was usually waiting at the foot of my bed, ready for his breakfast.

When he didn't come, I started to look in my closets and cupboards, since he frequently got himself stuck in random drawers while exploring. When I still couldn't find him, I got off the phone with Patty after it occurred to me that maybe, when I ordered my dinner the night before, Bug had managed to sneak out the door when the delivery person arrived. I grabbed my keys, went into the hallway, and started to call his name.

I became convinced that someone had heard his meows out there and stolen my little baby for themselves. I began to crawl up and down the hall on my hands and knees, peering through the cracks under my neighbors' doors while whispering as loudly as I dared into each apartment: *"Buuug! Buuug!"*

No luck. Then it occurred to me that someone might have found him and taken him down to the lobby so the front desk could watch over him until his owner came looking. I felt a wave of relief. That must be it. *Poor little guy, I hope he isn't too scared.* I rode the elevator down to the first floor, excited for our reunion and already planning the reward I'd give to whoever had been on duty and took care of him for me. The elevator doors opened, and I approached the woman sitting behind the front desk.

"Good morning! Did someone turn in my black cat? I think he got out into the hallway last night."

Her smile disappeared and her eyes widened in sadness and fear. It was that look someone gives before delivering awful, life-altering news.

"Early this morning . . . we found a black cat on the street," she stammered. "It seemed like he'd fallen." She didn't even have to say that he was dead. It was written all over her face.

Everything went dark for a moment. I felt my knees buckle, and as I bent over, the events from the previous night began to play out so clearly in my mind—the broken air conditioner's light flashing, opening the windows . . . How could I have been so stupid?

I began to wail as my legs fully gave out. The wail turned into a full-on scream as I curled up in the fetal position on the lobby floor.

The poor attendant came out from behind her desk and approached me cautiously. "Do you need help getting back upstairs? Is there someone I can call?"

I heard the elevator ding, and an elderly gentleman and his dog, on their way out for a morning walk, maneuvered their way around my crumpled body. Even through my hysterical state I could see the absurdity, almost as if I were floating above my body and watching myself writhe on the floor of the lobby in a busy apartment building at 7:30 a.m.

That's when a strangely calm and rational voice inside reminded me that I needed to be at work in two hours.

I collected myself up off the floor, thanked the woman for her help, and headed for the elevators. When I entered my apartment, the first thing I saw were all the cupboards and closets standing wide-open, a stark reminder that just twenty minutes earlier I'd thought Bug the Second was simply hiding. I couldn't fathom how my world had shifted so drastically in such a short amount of time, and that brought on a whole new wave of sobbing. There was nothing I wanted more than to take a mental health day from work to deal with the hideous mix of emotions washing over me—grief over Bug's death, guilt about how easily preventable it had been, and self-loathing from my unintentional role in it.

I saw the window, still open just a crack, but apparently wide enough for Bug to have squeezed through. I rushed across the room and pressed my mouth out into the open air. I tried to push the glass open wider, but it wouldn't budge, and I couldn't figure out how my cat had managed to wiggle through such a tight space.

"How could I be so stupid?" I screamed. I ranted into the air about what a terrible cat parent I was, screams that turned into unintelligible moans. I made the mistake of looking at the ledge outside the window, and could make out little claw marks in the city grime that had built up on the narrow space.

I pictured him scrambling to hold on as he slipped, and I began beating my face with my palms, imagining how scared he must have been. I sobbed with a primal rage I'd never experienced before.

Eventually I pulled my face back in and sank to the floor. My heart felt shattered, but I knew the clock was still ticking and the rational business side of my brain took over again. Maybe it was the denial stage of grief kicking in, mixed with some sort of internal coping mechanism, but I decided my emotions weren't what mattered in that moment.

The shoot scheduled for that morning was one of the most important ones that happens during a season—the end scene, with the whole *Queer Eye* team in our loft headquarters, watching and reacting as our hero takes all the things we've shown them and applies our suggestions to a big event in their lives. Normally, these days are so exciting, because it's our first chance to see the people we've been getting to know take to their new looks, their new skills, their newly designed environments, all on their own without our watchful eyes. It's even more fun to watch the heroes respond to their friends' and families' joy and amazement at the transformations.

These reveal days are a seriously big deal on the shooting schedule. People's jobs depended on me being there. To add to the pressure, we also happened to be hosting some contest winners whose prize had been to visit the loft and watch us film.

Committing to a television series, deciding to write a memoir, and booking a comedy tour all at once had finally caught up with me. I'd been able to juggle all of it so far, but losing a loved one so unexpectedly and in such a traumatic way, well, nobody knows what that feels like unless you've lived it. My work ethic felt utterly maxed out, but still, thoughts of all the time and labor our crew was putting in to make that day possible felt too big to ignore. I knew I had to consider their jobs too. Not to mention my castmates and, most important, our heroes.

Time felt like it was speeding up. I now had little over an hour to be dressed and ready on set, to turn on the effervescent JVN everyone knows and expects to see. There was no time to process this grief; my only choice was to try and bury enough of it to cope. I knew there was no way I could just waltz onto the set, though, pretending everything was fine, so I did what any *Downton Abbey* fan would do: I dressed all in black and left the building as a proper lady in mourning.

I'd called our showrunner before I left the apartment so she could let my castmates know about Bug the Second's untimely passing. I wanted them to be prepared for any morbid jokes I might blurt out as another element of my coping process. When I arrived, each of them was so understanding, giving me both the companionship and space that I required to do my job as professionally as possible. (Even after I gently stroked Tan's sweater-blouse and forlornly mentioned it looked just like the one my grandmother had been buried in.)

Looking back on those episodes now, I can see why people on Twitter were making snarky comments about my glassy-eyed look and lack of enthusiasm. I wasn't at one hundred per-cent, but I think I did my best with all things considered. I also know that by putting myself in the public eye, I open myself up to criticism. It's part of the business, and I get that, even if all I'm trying to do on *Queer Eye* is make people feel bet-ter about themselves. But before you publicly bash someone's appearance or behavior, try to remember: if someone seems off their game, there's probably a pretty good reason, so think twice before you say hateful things that you don't have the full story on.

I was able to make it through that shoot with the support of everyone there, but as we approached wrapping up filming for the day a horrible thought dawned on me. I'd been wait-ing to be done with work so I could take time off to properly mourn my cat, but I realized I literally had no time to take *any* days off. My schedule was booked solid, and getting some alone time to process the loss of my baby would be impossi-ble. So I made the very stable-genius decision to immediately fill the Bug the Second–shaped hole in my heart by invoking the *Charlotte's Web* rule again and impulse-adopting two new kittens.

I didn't even bother going back to my apartment first. I headed straight to the Philadelphia SPCA with my agent friend who'd come straight to the Philly set from Manhattan when she heard the news. She wanted to be there for me, and thank God she was.

When we walked into the rescue center, I immediately spotted a little tortoiseshell whom I instantly knew belonged to me. Any cat that cute had to be magic, which is why I promptly named her after the heroine in Roald Dahl's classic novel.

Hello, Matilda, I thought as I tickled the tiny tortie's face between the bars of her cage.

The only other kittens at the adoption center were black ones, which felt like a divine sign from the universe. *Yes, perfect*, I thought. *I'll adopt Bug the Third!* I'd fully turned into my grandparents, and I pictured a cycle of Bugs continuing on through my life until the end. (At least *my* version of replicating the same pet over and over again would acknowledge the ones that came before.)

I asked to hold a potential Bug the Third, but the moment the soft ball of fur was in my arms I began to weep. The woman working at the shelter looked concerned and stepped forward to take the kitten away.

"It's too soon after the accident for another black cat," I blurted out as I handed them back. Alarm spread over her face at the word "accident," and I realized that my uncontrollable crying probably wasn't giving her much confidence in me as a pet owner either.

My agent took the lady aside and quietly explained what had happened. She approached me after, and I was convinced she was going to say, "Hon, there is no way we are letting you take one of our cats today."

Instead, she hugged me and said that accidents happen, and it didn't make me a bad cat parent. She said in Philadelphia it happens a handful of times a year, and in other urban areas too. You just have to be careful of windows. It was something I hadn't considered until that morning, but listening to her affirm that I wasn't the worst idiot of all time was important. Those words were exactly what I'd needed to hear. Everyone had been so kind with their condolences, but what tugged below my grief was a fear that I wasn't fit to parent any pets. I hugged her back tightly and thanked her.

"My boyfriend is bringing over three kittens we've been fostering at home for a little while if you want to wait around," she told me. She'd barely finished the sentence before the bell above the door chimed and a guy walked in carrying a big cage.

For the next forty-five minutes I played with the three new kittens as my agent phoned Patty. After Patty arrived, they tried to talk me out of adopting all three of them, on top of Matilda. With Harry Larry at home and Liza eventually coming back from my mom's house once her digestive issues were settled, that would bring me to a grand total of six cats.

I finally listened to reason and chose only one from the new batch of three, keeping to my *Charlotte's Web* rule of two. The one I picked, Genevieve (as I would go on to name her), was a flame-point Siamese they'd found on the side of the street with her two brothers, and I breathed a small internal sigh of relief that I wasn't destined to turn into my grandparents after all. Once all the paperwork had been filed, I made my way home with Matilda, since Genevieve needed to stay an extra couple of days so she could be spayed.

I'll never forget walking into my apartment with Matilda. I took her into the bathroom to set up her kitten base camp so Harry Larry could get used to her presence and scent through the closed door before I officially introduced them. Once inside, I broke down in tears yet again. The cabinet doors were still open from my earlier searching, and as I looked at my new bundle of joy, this little soul I'd just agreed to protect, I felt a nauseating sense of guilt. How could I already love her so much right after losing Bug the Second?

Here's the thing about grief, though. There's no wrong way to express it, as long as your actions aren't causing harm to yourself or others. I needed something to help me get through that loss right then, and ever since my original Bug, I've found raising cats to be healing and comforting, and it gives me a sense of stability. With the immediate adoption, I was coping with my loss in the only way I knew how. Better yet, the process served to rescue two little kittens.

I think about that day a lot, though. I don't regret my decision to immediately adopt, at all, but I do wonder if there'd been any other ways I could have dealt with the loss to help me move forward. Because, to be perfectly honest, I'm still not completely over it. There are times when I can still feel the pure despair of seeing the claw marks on the windowsill where Bug the Second fell. I find myself wondering how long he'd been stuck out there before it happened. Had he been scared, or was it quick? Had he been meowing for me to come rescue him and I hadn't heard? I'll think of all the things I could have done differently, starting with not opening that fucking window, and berate myself for my decision to bring the cats back and forth from my New York City apartment to Philly, instead of just leaving them in New York, where Bug the Second would have been safe. At my apartment there, I had a protected little outdoor space where he could sit. Had he been confused in Philadelphia and just trying to get out to what he thought was the same place?

Writing about it now makes all of those feelings fresh again. My inwardly directed sadness and anger are still so strong. I wonder if I had allowed myself to sit with those feelings of grief for a while, instead of distracting myself after the accident, if I would still have these intense moments of pain.

I'll never know, but given who I am, I'm pretty sure there's nothing I could have done differently. Losing the original Bug, a thirteen-year-old cat I'd grown up with, had been gut-wrenching. But with him, I'd gotten a chance to say goodbye, to make sure he knew how much I loved him, and that comforted me. Losing Bug the Second so unexpectedly, when he was barely a year old, was a completely different kind of pain. A brutally sharp stab instead of a bittersweet ache. Everything I'd gone through while I was raising the first Bug—discovering my HIV status, a breakup with one of the loves of my life, losing my stepfather—all of that pain came rushing back in waves after Bug the Second's accident. The guilt I felt over his death brought up so much compounded shame and other losses in my life that I hadn't even realized I was still internally processing.

It's only in hindsight and through lots of self-work that I can have this perspective. I've been to rehab twice, weekly therapy ever since, and read everything Elisabeth Kübler-Ross ever wrote on grief, so I've learned a thing or two about the ways it works.

My therapist taught me about something called our "window of tolerance," which is essentially the space wherein a person is able to function the most effectively amid the regular stresses of everyday life—the times between moments of extreme stress, acute reactions, or emotional numbness brought on by trauma.

In that narrow space between losing Bug the Second and adopting Matilda and Genevieve, my window of tolerance was stretched so thin it was probably see-through. I may not have been acting within a rational frame of mind, but ultimately, I have to tell myself that I did the right thing for me at that moment.

I realize having your cat fall out of a high-rise window is not necessarily a universal experience. But we've all been devastated by the loss of someone close to us, and it brings to light another major thing I've learned about grief: that it can exist only in the presence of deep and pure love. The whole "Better to have loved and lost" saying is a cliché, but there is a kind of radical Buddhist acceptance to acknowledge: that allowing yourself to love another human or a pet is a huge risk, because nothing is permanent. When we make a conscious decision to love, we're essentially also choosing to suffer. Every marriage will end in death or divorce. Every pet or friend we have in our life, we'll lose eventually, either to death, rehoming, or simply drifting apart.

That leaves two choices. You can build a wall around yourself, so you don't get attached to anything and live a cold, unfulfilling life. Or you take risks and love. You only live once (as far as I know), and a person can't be an island forever without making themselves more miserable than they would be if they chose to be vulnerable to connection.

All that said, my ways of grieving are certainly not right for everyone. There's no such thing. Between friends, family, coworkers, and social media, we all have opinions flying at us two ways from Sunday, and judgments from others can cloud the voice inside each of us that tells us what we really need. When I lost Bug the Second, my centered self—the part of me that chooses self-love instead of self-destruction—intuitively told me what I needed to get through the situation.

I think the only universal key to processing grief is to have compassion for yourself, to be able to ask yourself what it is *you* really need, and to not care about how others perceive your process. It's important to ask others for help if you need it, but it's *so* important to have the courage to ask *yourself* for help too. (Fast-forward thirty years and I'm living on a farm with three hundred cats, coping gorgeously while heading into the season 47 finale of *Hoarders*.)

CHAPTER 2

THE (CONTINUAL) EXPRESSION OF MY PERSONAL STYLE

*Or, what is it about impulse-buying luxury items that
makes me feel validated in the moment, but then totally
empty inside after I've blown thousands on a Bottega
Veneta garment that stays hidden in my closet for a year?*

There's a scene in the 1997 film *My Best Friend's Wedding* where Julia Roberts is getting fitted for a pale lavender, off-the-shoulder, draped silk crepe bridesmaid's dress. She's being forced to listen to Cameron Diaz drag on about how in love she is with her fiancé, who happens to be Julia's titular best friend. Julia has finally realized that she's also bone-crushingly, butt-hungrily in love with that stunner of a '90s leading man, Dermot Mulroney. Albeit it's a jealousy-driven love, but love all the same.

Right as Julia steps off the fitting stand, her bent leg rips a foot-long tear in the dress's seam. The moment is played for laughs, but to my ten-year-old self, there was not one damn thing funny about it *at all*. In fact, I gasped out loud and nearly shit my pants. Knowing even at that young age that bridesmaids' gowns are usually a catastrophe, this smoky lilac dress was an exception to the rule, fit for Lady Diana herself. How could Julia have been so careless? Looking back, I can pinpoint that exact moment as my first realization of just how much fashion means to me. If Julia's gown was flawless enough to potentially win the affection of Dermot Mulroney (her gay bff, played by Rupert Everett, approved of it as well), its power of persuasion drove home the idea that when we look stunning, we are confident and able to do anything we set our minds to. Even if that means breaking Cameron Diaz's heart, ruining a wedding that cost hundreds of thousands of dollars, and nearly causing untold fatalities throughout downtown Chicago. But it's all worth it when we feel amazing in our couture!

I already knew by then that I loved style and all things glamour. I'd memorized every sequin on the black and gold dress Kristi Yamaguchi wore while skating for her gold medal at the 1992 Olympics. But my full-body emotional reaction to seeing such a gorgeous creation carelessly torn apart just because Julia got angsty for a cigarette (ew, yes, I'm an ex–cigarette smoker, and everyone knows we are the worst) made me realize that my passion for fashion went much deeper than mere starry-eyed appreciation.

From there, I started paying closer attention to the kinds of clothes I was drawn to. Yes, silhouettes were important, but I began to realize there was so much more to clothing! Color, texture, patterns, and prints were all part of the experience, and even though I couldn't quite articulate it at the time, I knew that the garments I was most drawn to—feminine and unique—represented something deep within me and held power that could be used for self-expression beyond words.

Not that I could just snap my fingers and parade around in the clothes that I gravitated towards. Growing up a young queer child in a small midwestern city had already brought up enough challenges when it came to gender expression. Whenever my family caught five-year-old me playing dress-up with my cousins, wearing all of their awe-inspiring little-girl gowns (or even just my preferred tights and Barney-print off-the-shoulder sweatshirt frocks at home), they were not happy. My femininity on full display was not something anyone celebrated except me. My father seared it into my brain that tights, evening gowns, skirts, and sequins were not for boys, and I needed to banish my desire to wear them. Dress-up got shut down, and the people closest to me remained blind to the pain I was experiencing not only from the shaming of my young exploration of gender expression and later sexual orientation but also from being sexually abused and keeping it a secret. I was already something unfamiliar, they didn't recognize any of the warning signs that I had started to retreat deep into my mind. Some of my coping mechanisms were unhealthy, but others fueled my imagination. I might have been forbidden to express myself the way I wanted, but that didn't stop me from being an enthusiastic spectator on the fashion sidelines as I grew into my tweens and teens.

I especially loved reading fashion magazines. We didn't fly very often, but whenever we did, I'd beg my mother for money at the airport so I could buy *Vogue*, *Harper's Bazaar*, or *Vanity Fair*. The pages became doorways to fantasy worlds that transported me far away from Quincy, Illinois, my hometown, to places where everyone had perfect hair, perfect makeup, and stunning clothes, where women swanned around ancient ruins and posed on mountaintops, draped in fabulous jewels, sunlight glinting off their perfectly dewy skin.

Who created these magnificent scenes? I had to know. Was it all an act? Or were these worlds still somehow attainable if I coupled my blind ambition with enough hard work. Maybe someday I could make like Ariel and be a part of their world. I tried to memorize the names of all the designers mentioned, as well as the names of the makeup artists, models, and stylists listed in tiny print and buried in the margins. I vowed that one day I'd not only be involved in building these elaborate fantasies but make them become my real world as well. That lady wearing six-inch heels and a boa while high stepping through a steaming lava field? If I ever got to go hiking in Hawaii, that's how I was going to do it too.

Sticker shock would always rocket me back to reality. Four-hundred-dollar jeans? A seven-hundred-dollar sweater? Three thousand dollars for a coat and six thousand dollars for a bag? On what planet does that exist, and when will I get there? The first time I saw those numbers I thought they were typos, that someone had fallen asleep on their keyboard and hit the zero button a few too many times before sending the pages off to the printer. I was constantly gobsmacked by the prices, and then I'd get lost in a pit of depression because I'd remember that even if I did work hard enough to ever afford the clothes, I wouldn't even be allowed to do anything with them since it was constantly drilled into my head that boys don't carry purses, or rock heels, or wear any of the works of art on those pages that I felt so naturally a part of.

The only time I'd ever seen men in women's clothing was the time that *South Park*'s Matt Stone and Trey Parker dressed up in iconic Oscars looks from J.Lo and Gwyneth Paltrow when they went to the Academy Awards, which the world would later learn they were attending while tripping their faces off on acid.

It was all considered a big joke, obviously nothing to ever be taken seriously. The world of high fashion felt like a sandbox I was never going to get to play in.

Halloween was an exception. Finally a society-sanctioned opportunity to explore my fabulous woman within, usually by donning one of my great-grandmother's vintage dresses for trick-or-treating, my hair wrapped in a scarf, looking like a white, prepubescent Miss Cleo. My mom would take me from house to house for candy, because even though I felt like I had the confidence of a young Liza Minnelli, there was no way I was going to hang solo with the neighborhood kids dressed like a lady.

I worked this costume a few years in a row until the stares I started to get from strangers and family alike became scarier than any monster costume. As I approached my teens, people's disgusted reactions outweighed the joy I got from wearing a dress. Rather than risk making the other 364 days of the year miserable for myself, I decided it was best to let the holiday go.

But it wasn't just about people's reactions. I gave up on that side of myself because of all the not-so-subtle cues I had started to receive from guys as I hit puberty. Being the butt of jokes from other boys in my school because I was feminine and chubby became more than just an attack on how I felt about myself: if I ever wanted to do anything with all of the intense desires my budding homo hormones were suddenly conjuring up, I knew I'd better shut that side of myself away for good, because it became abundantly clear nobody was interested in a femme boy.

This was true even in openly gay spaces outside the bubble of my small town and school. Before Grindr and SCRUFF, queer boys with internet access had Gay.com and AOL gay chat rooms, which I would frequent in the relentless pursuit of validation I wanted but never received in real life. But I quickly learned that there's so much internalized misogyny and homophobia within the gay community, I needed to hide who I was there too. The language was all right there on the dating sites and in the chat rooms waiting for me as I began to become sexually active:

> Masc 4 Masc.
> No femmes.
> Does your voice sound gay?
> Dude, are you wearing tights in that pic?

I've always known I didn't feel completely male or female, but in those early days of having gay men reject me because of my femininity, I learned fast to masculinize. If the gay community was forcing me to choose between a blow job and Balenciaga (if I could afford it), the bj was still gonna win every time.

Well, at least until my late twenties, when I'd sucked so many dicks there was a comma in the number. Frankly, my validation that I could get laid any time I wanted had been quenched, but my sense of self had not. I didn't think anyone would ever love my true feminine queer self.

The clash between my style predilections and how they were received by the guys I wanted to bump uglies with caused a long detour off the road to finding my true style. But even if I had met a hot dude who was down to plow me under seven layers of pink tulle, I couldn't have afforded it back then. As I got into hairdressing, cute clothes were not in the cards, let alone high fashion.

After moving to Arizona, renting a chair at a salon for the first time, building a clientele, and paying rent, fast fashion became the way to go for me. I lived in Zara and I loved it. But when it came to sex, pretending to be butch was my top priority. For every bedazzled pair of tights I snuck into my closet at home, there was also a pair of cut-off jeans and a solid color tightish T-shirt for my nights out cruising, so that other men would find me masculine enough. I had to hide my heels or risk my dick appointment scattering away.

I know I often make jokes to bring lightness to a sad situation, but the reality here is that I was downplaying my femininity at the expense of expressing my true self at the salon, out in my social life, and in my sex life. I felt that being masculine was the key to success in finding love, and that's sad. So many people in the gay male community find themselves trying to stifle their femme nature to be more desirable and try to avoid the casual cruelty so often flung between gay men and queer people.

But as the years went on and I moved to Los Angeles, I began to grow more self-confident and got more comfortable with my femininity. I knew that creatively I wasn't living my best fashion life, but in the privacy of my own home I could wear—and act—however I wanted. I wasn't exactly making bank, so I'd go to Payless to purchase heels that I could practice walking around the house in. My shorts got shorter, my shirts got cropped, and little by little I started to blossom. I always thought LA had just rubbed its Hollywood-esque nature off on me and allowed me to further embrace my fabulousness, but looking back, I can see that I came into my own style-wise at the same time that I had reached an emotional maturity I'd fought hard to attain. During this stage, my primary focus was recovering from my drug and sex addictions and getting myself back into a healthy mental state. Once my life and career started to stabilize in my mid- to late twenties, I began to get even more comfortable playing around with the feminine side of myself that I'd hidden for so long.

I bought more Payless heels, but instead of simply miming a catwalk across my living room during the commercials of

America's Next Top Model, I started to learn elaborate Beyoncé dance routines from one of my best friends. I'd wear those heels, a crop top, and some Tina Turner gold tights. Sometimes we'd pop out to El Pollo Loco to get a snack afterwards, with me still in my choreo-learning outfit. Look at me thriving in my authenticity and no one chasing me out of the restaurant! I got into wearing sparkly bright American Apparel tights, which made me feel like a powerful '80s aerobics instructor. It finally seemed like I was starting to live my best *full* life, because my desire to express my true self became greater than my need for sexual validation. It felt great to not need to butch it up to go out anymore, and a general sense of ease, acceptance, and playfulness started to swell inside.

I was no longer relapsing on drugs and digging myself out of the financial holes my benders always left me in. I'd found therapy, recovery programs, including twelve-step and group work, as well as harm reduction tools, all of which gave me the strength to work through the sexual compulsivity with a side of meth addiction that had plagued me in the past. Suddenly, rocking the clothes that made me feel my best was something that also helped in my recovery. Finding myself desirable and worthy of attention in whatever I chose to wear lifted my blinders. I had been conforming to what I thought people wanted, which had left me feeling empty. What once had been my insecurity began to become a source of strength. We love!

Ironically, the thing I always thought would hold me back in life became a catalyst for me achieving the kind of success I had never even dreamed of. I starred in a cult classic comedic web series called *Gay of Thrones*, in which I was completely and outrageously myself. And after I booked *Queer Eye*, I suddenly found myself in a position to afford all of those astronomically priced clothes I'd coveted as a child, as well as an apartment with big closets to put them in. I'd gone through the looking glass and become one of the beautiful people in the magazines I used to love, peering out instead of in, covered in high fashion and even higher price tags.

My shopping lust knew no bounds as I scooped up entire racks of Rick Owens. Maison Margiela? Yes, one of each, please. Chanel pumps that were twice my rent? *Duh!* There was one Bottega Veneta bag that cost so much it honestly makes me ashamed to say I bought it. (No, I'm not telling you how much.)

And who knew Mary-Kate and Ashley Olsen would continue ruining my life after childhood? Back then my trauma had come from realizing I'd never have a twin after watching *It Takes Two*. As an adult, they cursed me again with their genius fashion line The Row and my discovery of the most fucking chic and simple, perfect and lovely, but literally eight-thousand-dollar column dress. Yes, bitch, I need three. Whoooo am IIIIIIII?????

I hate people like me, but I am one. The purchases I made brought me joy at first, but I eventually discovered that shopping for luxury items shares a lot of parallels with drug addiction.

Except it doesn't! Because meth is bad and clothes are *gooooood.*

Omg, see what I mean??

First comes the craving. (*I want this and will do anything to get my hands on it.*)

That's followed by giddy fear, anticipation, internal bargaining and justification, and acceptance of truth. (*Am I about to drop six thousand dollars on a coat? It's discounted from nine thousand dollars, so it would be irresponsible not to buy it. Oh noooo, I am a clothes addict!*)

There's the rush of the purchase itself (*Omg, I did it!*), the thrilling narcissistic possession high (*Mine, mine, mine!*), followed by an inevitable crash (*Dear Jesus, what have I done to my bank account? You're so selfish! People are suffering and now you have four cashmere crop-top turtleneck sweaters! And they're all cream!*).

Shopping sprees can even breed the same kind of sneaky secrecy that drugs create. I found myself buying expensive things, hiding them deep in my closet, and never telling anyone because I felt so guilty. I started obsessing over all the stuff that the money I'd just spent could do for others. I'd look at a new handbag and wonder if the cash I'd spent could feed a struggling family or help a sick kid. And then I'd buy it anyway.

I started to apply some of the work I'd done in therapy to psychologize my shopping habits and how they made me feel. On the one hand, I was literally wrapping myself in my childhood dreams, but on the other, I was also cloaked in all of my childhood anxiety, fear, and shame. There were so many times in my life when I thought I'd never make it, when I didn't believe in myself and figured I'd never be able to afford all the treasures I saw in magazines. I couldn't understand why I gave so much power to objects that made me feel so terrible, and my brain would run in circles:

Fuck you, world, I made it despite everything you threw at me, and these clothes are proof!

Followed by: *Holy shit, Jonathan, you are smarter than this.*

And then: *But omg, this scarf is so soft and pretty, and nobody else makes clothes as timeless and well-constructed as The Row, and I can leave it to my godchild in my will.*

And then that thought would lead me right back to *Fuck you, world, I made it.*

Is this the arena where I've placed a lot of my self-validation? If I can understand all the things that are wrong with a meaningless hunt for high fashion, why do I still pursue it? I'm not going to lie—I've gotten better about shopping, but I do still sometimes make some obscene splurges. The truth is, the desire for luxury fashion was imprinted on me at such a young age that I still find it hard to shake. While growing up, I felt so undesirable, and while grappling with both my gender identity and sexual orientation, I was always looking for the magic fix to all my problems. Fashion was a big one. I thought that if only I looked better, people would want to be nice to me. In reality, people can still be shitty no matter what I'm wearing. (Even though around the time I discovered this I was wearing an American Apparel circle scarf.)

Still, there's a part of me that can't quite let go of the harmful lesson I took from those magazines: that if I couldn't afford their clothes, then I was simply never going to be as carefree and fuckable as their perfect models. Back then, imagining a future for myself when I could be like those women wearing gorgeous pieces would end in a resounding *no*, but now my wallet can say *yes*. And God, does she love to say yes.

I absolutely get that it's up to me to untie this psychological knot, and since awareness is the first step, I'm on my way there. I can see the areas where my fashion-addict self is doing better and taking my own advice—that just because I can doesn't mean I should. And I'm constantly learning that my actions and spending habits influence more than just my bank account. While I don't want to sound preachy, it is pretty awful how the financial side of fashion can so deeply affect people's self-confidence, particularly in the LGBTQIA+

community. I think things are slowly changing for the better, but when I was still searching for self-worth in fashion magazines, there wasn't a ton of emphasis on self-love, inclusivity, or self-acceptance in those pages. And I'm hardly the first young queer who has been drawn to fashion magazines at an impressionable moment.

But hidden inside that fantasy world, unhealthy doubts about our ability to become self-sufficient start to take root. (Similar in some ways to how unrealistic body representation and standardized beauty ideals cause so much psychological damage in young people.) Oftentimes people become so seduced by magazine fashion and the labels their celebrity idols wear that they go deep into debt trying to emulate an exterior that presents itself as self-expression, but in reality, it's just clothing, none of which really translates to our quality of life. It's obvious that the clothes in magazines are too expensive for anyone who isn't as rich as a motherfucker. But even if someone is rich enough to afford them, does that make them happy? I wish I'd spent more time thinking about that question when I was a kid.

Honestly, I could also stand to do some reflection on it as an adult. After yet another impulse-spending romp at Bergdorf Goodman in the summer of 2019, I forced myself to face that the emptiness I felt afterwards was three doors down from what I used to feel after sexually acting out. (Minus the chlamydia.)

It made me realize I needed to start asking myself some more questions.

What's beneath the need to go impulse shopping? Was I feeling lonely? Was I still trying to prove something to an insecure part of myself? Was it a control issue?

I didn't like a lot of the answers I came up with at first. Many times they weren't even answers, just half-formed thoughts that I'd quickly bury so I could get that Bottega jacket onto my body ASAP. But I think the question about control hits closest to home. Part of me tried to convince myself that shopping just felt good and it wasn't hurting anyone, but another part knew that I was being driven by a need to feel in control of a new life that made me feel out of control.

After I developed a greater sense of self-awareness about my own issues with style and spending, I pushed myself harder, forcing myself to look at the fashion industry's many flaws. There's so much wasteful excess! The BBC reported that 85 percent of all textiles in the US—more than fourteen million tons in 2017 alone—is burned or dumped in landfills.[1] It's estimated that 35 percent of microplastic pollution found in the ocean comes from textiles' synthetic microfibers.[2] The animal cruelty in the fur industry is unforgivable. And according to *Forbes*, the fashion industry is the second largest polluter of freshwater resources on the planet.[3]

I'm not going to sit here and pretend that I know all of

the evils committed by the fashion industry. In fact, I'm sure Greta Thunberg would rip this chapter out and shove it up my nostrils before schooling me on the rest of the damage that's happening to Parent Earth because of fashion. But so many problematic industries are set up in a way to make us think that we have no method to positively influence things, and that's simply not true. Supply and demand is still a thing, and if we're more aware of our actions, we can make better choices.

Once I learned this, whenever I got the urge to spend, I started opening my wallet to designers like Stella McCartney, who has been extremely vocal about her anti-fur policies ever since she started her brand. I looked to celebrities like Tiffany Haddish and Kate Middleton for inspiration, since they were recycling clothes they'd worn before to big events—something that once was considered a fashion sin of the highest order. They broke down that bullshit barrier, and Tiffany remained her hilarious self and Kate stayed a prim and proper princess. So do I need a new pair of shoes for everything? No. Can I werk a red carpet in the same garment twice? Hell yes! I realized I don't need all new clothes for every single interview, TV show, or press junket. I can re-wear all sorts of stuff, and nobody is gonna get hurt.

Lately, when I buy new clothes or shoes, I ask myself, *Who is this for? Me? My family, my friends? Is my butthole lonely? Is it for photographers on a red carpet? Does this piece of clothing make me feel good about myself? Am I trying to make others feel comfortable, or myself? How much longer until I lose all feeling in my feet from these heels?*

If I'm shopping online, I'll do some research about the brand and see what I can dig up about whether the company operates in a way that's in line with my own ethics. Do they support Black Lives Matter without trying to capitalize off the movement? Is their social media and advertising problematic in any way? Are any of the board members QAnon/lizard people believers? Or maybe even Trump supporters?

Nudism is totally fabulous if that's your truth, but in my case I need to buy and wear clothes, and that's most likely the case with you too. The things we wear send a message to the people around us; at the highest level, what we wear can become an elaborate form of self-expression, but even at its most basic, it's a way of telling the world how we want to be seen. As RuPaul said, "We're all born naked, and the rest is just drag." But fashion can also be a source of insecurity, a symbol of worth, and a comparative cudgel we use to relentlessly judge ourselves and one another.

Bringing a deeper awareness into my relationship with clothing—beyond a flash-point thought like *Does this make me look hot?*—has only made me a more caring and discerning person. No matter what's on my body, it's my heart, my curiosity, and my essence that make me unique. There's only one of me in the world, and that's what's truly valuable—not the price of what I'm wearing. I know because I've met an awful lot of folks over the years who wear expensive clothes, but what I quickly learned is that some of the chicest-looking people have the cheapest integrity. Even after all the work I've done, I still need to remind myself, almost every day, that our hearts are where the real couture is found.

CHAPTER 3

QUINCY'S QUEER HISTORY

*Or, how I learned to see the LGBTQIA+ support
community that exists in my hometown.*

I want to be one of those people who love the place they came from. A regular non-problematic Carrie Underwood singing "Thank God for Hometowns." Where you're from doesn't make you who you are, but it can certainly play a role in how you see yourself—and my hometown of Quincy, Illinois, did me little to no favors in the self-love department.

In addition to all of the trauma I experienced there, it was a daily struggle having to keep who I was bottled up inside (something that is clearly not my strong suit). And once I finally did start coming out to some friends and members of my family, certain people reacted as if I was the first effeminate, dick-loving person to emerge from the state.

As a young queer person in a seemingly straight-as-they-come town, there weren't any places I knew of to turn to for support. This was long before Gay-Straight Alliance groups became a fairly normal extracurricular club to join in high school. Who knows what would have happened had there been one when I was there—meeting weekly in a safe little room plastered with posters of Bette Midler, Cher, and Michelle Kwan. I might have ended up a Quincian for life! But there wasn't, and for the most part I felt completely alone and got the hell out of my small town the second I could.

Through the healing of distance and time, my heart has softened on Quincy. Having realized my dream of getting out, I began to wonder about the generations before me who hadn't had the resources to leave even if they'd wanted to. And people who made it *to* Quincy from someplace more rural, since at around forty thousand residents it's the biggest city for miles around. Had there been LGBTQIA+ generations before me who'd worked to foster a better existence for its community? And what about my LGBTQIA+ peers who still remain joyfully in Quincy today?

With all of these questions burning a hole in my top knot, I decided to make like Harriet the Spy, grab my notebook, and learn more about the queer history of my hometown.

I quickly uncovered a small but thriving LGBTQIA+ scene full of folks and community resources that had been in place for decades. What in the Adam Rippon is this?? I had no idea these people existed and quickly realized I needed to rewrite the narrative I'd scripted about my hometown, focusing more on the joy, bravery, and connection it contained rather than the neglect and abuse that had symbolized the place for most of my life.

I should give you a little history lesson before we dive in: Quincy is located right on the Mississippi River, a place where steamboats stopped and with a major railroad crossing. This means there have always been lots of people passing through for very short periods of time. According to Jason Lewton, editor of our town's newspaper, this is why our downtown area, which is only a couple of blocks from the river and the train tracks, had a long-held reputation as a place of ill repute. Or, as I call it, a place where you can bruise your knees while the warm humid air coming from the Mississippi River caresses your butt cheeks.

"There were brothels into the '50s," Jason divulged. "There was a rather vibrant red-light district throughout that area, and an adult movie theater. For a long time, this was a hangout for people from Chicago and a lot of factory workers. It was a heavy drinking town." Apparently, some people even called Quincy "Little Chicago" back in the day.[1]

The unofficial headquarters for queer people to meet and hang out was a hotel with a bar in the back, and honestly, the history of the building deserves its own book. The first iteration of it was called Quincy House. It opened in 1838 and was the cat's meow and where everyone who was anyone wanted to be, with a separate entrance for ladies so they wouldn't have to pass by the bar. Abraham Lincoln (*cough*–gay, look it up–*cough*) even came through a few times, once when he was in town for a debate. Quincy House burned down in 1883, then eventually got rebuilt as this huge Romanesque place with a tower and was renamed the Newcomb Hotel. It was just as fancy as the previous one and had a restaurant that served elevated ritzy fare like calves' brains and green sea turtle soup.

Gross.

Another fire broke out at the hotel in 1904 and killed a few people, but the hotel managed to stay open all the way through the mid-1980s. I wish I could've bumped uglies with an old-timey Chicago muscle daddy in the '60s, but alas, I was born right place, wrong time.

The discreet gay clientele who'd been meeting at that hotel's bar ditched it in 1976 for a place called The Main Drag, which was Quincy's first official gay bar. Normsie townsfolk assumed its name came from the fact that it was located on one of the town's main streets, but there were actual drag shows happening there, thanks to the bar's owner, a vintage drag queen named Willard Kaufman, who went by several different names–Willie to his friends, Irene West when dressed in drag, and Mother to all the people she took under her wing, which was pretty much any scared, closeted gay person from the Midwest timidly stepping into a gay bar for the very first time in their lives, many of whom had driven hours from the middle of nowhere to get there.

Irene took her drag name from two of her favorite people: the original Irene was an adored waitress who'd worked at that bar inside the Newcomb, and the last name was in honor of Mae West. This type of midwestern iconizing is what I'm talking about, honey! After running The Main Drag for a few years, Irene closed it and reopened another gay bar on New Year's Eve heading into 1981, called Irene's Cabaret. Okay, queer entrepreneurship in a city and time that didn't even want you to be there! Yes, resilience!

For most, Irene's Cabaret wasn't much to look at. It was a little brick building with a neon rainbow sign that seldom worked. But to me when I was growing up, Irene's was a beacon. The building was located across the street from the TV station my dad worked at, so every time I visited him there I'd say I wanted to take a look at the dance academy next door, but instead I'd stroll past Irene's. I knew exactly what that neon rainbow sign meant. It was a clue that maybe, just maybe, I would suck dick in this town someday. I was desperate to see a Cutie McCuterson walk in or out, but I never got a peek inside during my little stakeouts.

Apparently, I wasn't the only one curious about the place. Queer historian and writer Owen Keehnen describes the inside of Irene's this way in a tribute essay on his website that he wrote after discovering Irene's had closed down in 2016:

Irene's was a focal point for queer activity in the tri-state area. People would drive there from Keokuk and Springfield and Palmyra on the weekends. Irene's was a true melting pot of drag queens, leathermen, hustlers, lesbian farmers, bi-curious spouses, etc. Every combination of LGBT was represented at Irene's almost every night of the week. In the bar's crimson light we became comrades and friends and had a lot of fun. . . .

I went there in the first years it was in business, but even then the place looked as though it had been around for decades. The decor had a lived-in look. I remember the etched tin ceilings, the dim red lighting, red-flocked wallpaper, a David statue adorned with a boa, a disco ball, and mirrored walls. Overall, a sort of river boat brothel chic.

Beat-up tables and chairs surrounded the dance floor and to one side, a glowing diva-heavy jukebox—Della Reese, Dottie West, Blondie, Irene Cara, Patsy Cline, even Pia Zadora. On quiet nights at the bar Willie (aka Irene) would often hand me a few quarters[:]

"Hon, go play something on that thing to make me smile."[2]

BEFORE JASON LEWTON became the editor of Quincy's *Herald-Whig*, he actually worked part-time at Irene's Cabaret as a bartender. "You had to enter through the back door in the alley, so it wasn't that conspicuous," he said. Those directions even served as the bar's slogan, printed on matchbooks: "Enter in the Rear." (We midwestern queens are a resourceful and hilarious bunch.)

"I won't lie," Jason added. "It was kind of a cruising spot. But just being around people where you could feel free to be yourself isn't something you can always do in a small town. Particularly in Quincy, it was always difficult, because there's this urge here for everyone to fit in and conform and be part of what is 'normal' Quincy."[3]

One thing I've observed from hearing the stories of LGBTQIA+ people in small towns or rural cities in the US is that many feel they don't have any safe spaces or a chance to be welcomed into sought-after circles of "normal" people. Being dehumanized and pushed into the periphery of society will always feel strongly familiar to those of us who have lived that experience. And it's why we cherish the places that welcome us with open arms, which are quite often charming little dive bars.

What made Irene's Cabaret even more special was Irene's commitment to also creating a space for members of the LGBTQIA+ community who didn't drink and/or struggled with how the religion they'd been raised in made them feel about themselves. Because of this, she let a friend named Reid Christensen open a local chapter of a protestant Christian church specifically for LGBTQIA+ folks, called the Metropolitan Community Church, or MCC, right upstairs from the bar. If someone arrived at the bar seeking community but they weren't a drinker, they could go up there instead and meet and hang out with like-minded people.

This is *everything* to me. How ahead of their time could they be? Literally, this is like the sober queer-owned coffee shops and meeting spaces that usually could be found only in large cities. A Christian group with an actual acceptance of LGBTQIA+ folks!? Roundhouse kick to those tacky "God Hates Fags" poster-carrying, bad-perm-having Westboro Baptist church members.

"The Quincy group had the best tone of any of the churches I was associated with," remembered Roy Birchard, an MCC pastor who traveled around from church to church and spent time with the congregation in the '80s. At the time there were about forty-four regular members. "And it was because of Reid. He modeled and promoted warm, loving, and kind relationships to a degree that was remarkable. I once wrote a tribute to it for the MCC theological journal and described going there as feeling like stepping into a warm bath, or a sauna if you came in from the outside. It just made you feel good, and people flourished."[4]

This was hardly a feeling that a queer person could expect from whatever church they'd been raised in, which is commonplace in many churches around the world but especially small-town USA. MCC's work highlights the uniqueness, nerve, and heart it took to recognize the human need for a spiritual and person-affirming community for LGBTQIA+ people in little Quincy, Illinois. Learning about this gives me so much pride in the local queer heroes who have done so much more for me than I ever knew. As tough as Quincy could be for LGBTQIA+ residents, it would've been even tougher without places like this.

* * *

In a cruel coincidence, the year that Irene's Cabaret opened, 1981, was also the year AIDS made its official horrifying debut. Or, as doctors called it back then, GRID, which stood for gay-related immunodeficiency. Safe spaces for queer people became even more essential as waves of a familiar homophobia became more rampant but this time mixed with a new hyper-religious, end-of-days, God-is-punishing-gay-people narrative that was (and still is) uniquely damaging.

As AIDS began killing more and more people throughout the early '80s, there was a lot of disgusting misinformation flying around, like how it was a plague sent by God to condemn homosexuality or that you'd catch it if you swam in the same pool as an HIV+ person. And forget kissing or sharing a drink—you'd be doomed.

Unless you were in the thick of it, all anyone really saw of the disease was evening news footage of anonymous skeletal men in hospital beds. But on July 25, 1985, HIV/AIDS found a public face when Rock Hudson announced he was suffering from the disease, which created heightened awareness around the epidemic.

For those who aren't familiar, Rock was a mega celeb, a major leading man at the time. Think Brad Pitt-level fame, and someone who managed to hold on to his heartthrob status for over three decades while remaining in the closet. I hope he at least got to get dicked down by some hotties while the going was good, but I digress.

Rock also happened to be a close friend of Nancy Reagan's, one of the ultimate OG Karens, and she rejected a plea from him in his dying days when he was trying to seek treatment in Paris. A call from the White House would have helped him obtain the hospital transfer he needed, but she turned him down under the guise of not doing anything that would "favor personal friends," as one White House staffer later phrased it.[5]

I'm sure a political historian could trace much bigger favors given to other special friends who weren't seeking treatment for an illness completely stigmatized by the Reagans and so many of their Christian, right-wing, morally hypocritical voters. It took another two years after Rock's death, which was on October 2, 1985, before Ronald even mentioned AIDS in a press conference. The bungling of and lack of attention paid to the HIV/AIDS epidemic resulted in hundreds of thousands of deaths. It's astounding to me that by the end of 1985, the reported AIDS cases in America had increased by 89 percent compared to 1984, and it's worth noting again that the president did not so much as mention it for another two years. To this day, for many Americans his polished image covers up a massive atrocity that's hard to wrap your head around.

I want to take a moment here to send love to all the folks we lost at the hands of a government that did not even pretend to care about them. You were loved, and we won't forget you.

I bring all of this up because the day before Rock died, a woman named Carleen Orton came to work at the Adams County Health Department, which is based in Quincy. She'd been hired to coordinate maternity/child health nursing, but during that first week of media hype around Rock's death, her boss told her they wanted her to step in and become their AIDS coordinator instead.

"The first thing we wanted to do was set up a testing site,

because there wasn't one available before that," Carleen said. "Donated blood was being tested for HIV, so some people were donating blood to try and find out if they were HIV positive that way, thinking, *Well, I'll get notified if I'm positive.* We needed testing that was secure and anonymous so we could reach at-risk people." Carleen was able to convince the state health department to help set up a hotline that people could call. They were given a code number that could be used as personal identification for testing and counseling, instead of being forced to give their name. Her system began being used across the whole state. We see you, resourceful clever Carleen, kicking ass and saving lives!

Carleen organized a task force that met monthly, and it included local doctors, school administrators, people who worked in infection control at the Red Cross, and even funeral home owners. Everyone would share any new information they'd learned and brainstorm new ways to increase testing, raise awareness, educate, and destigmatize HIV and AIDS. I cannot even fathom how many roadblocks and how much cruelty Carleen must have run into setting all this up, which makes it even more inspiring that she didn't stop.

It was fairly easy for the task force to do outreach at drug treatment centers and in recovery programs, but men having sex with men was a high-risk community that Carleen knew she needed to connect with, and she didn't know how to. So she got the pastor of MCC at the time to join their group, and he helped her start making inroads with Quincy's hidden gay community, men who could educate her about the lifestyle and risks people were taking.

She remembered that when the pastor took her to MCC for the first time so she could give a talk about the testing and counseling services the Adams County Health Department provided, the group was a mix of regular churchgoers and people who had come upstairs from the bar. "We did the education, the safe-sex lecture, handed out condoms."[6]

I cannot impress upon you just how revolutionary this was to do in Quincy in the '80s. These people were breaking new ground and risking relationships to help some of the most vilified members of our community.

Carleen continued her AIDS work and outreach until she retired in 1996 and a new nurse, Karen Spring, took over her role. "We had to write grants every year to get our testing equipment and condoms," Karen remembered. She wanted to create an incentive for more gay men to get tested and wrote a grant that allowed her to buy Visa gift cards to hand out in exchange.

Her hope was to get testing started on-site at Irene's, since even with anonymous testing, gay men still had to show their faces at the health department at the time, and many were too scared to be seen there because of AIDS being so stigmatized. Irene was more than happy to let Karen start offering free

HIV testing at the bar. Karen's grant also got her some money to pay a well-liked bar patron and member of the Quincy gay community to put up notices at the bar ahead of time and talk to people about why it was important to get tested. Basically, she hired a PR man for her semimonthly testing nights, which is a genius move, in my mind, that showcases ways in which mutual aid and personal resourcefulness fills the void government inaction leaves.

"We'd always go around and talk to as many people as we could in the bar first, and back in the day it was always very, very crowded," she recalled. "There was a dance floor and games in the back, and there was comradery. Irene would grab me and kiss me every time I came in! She made it so comfortable for new people, because a lot would come from miles around and they had no idea what was going on. They knew that they were gay, but they had no idea what 'gay' really meant. Irene sat at the bar every night in her later days, and people would come up to her with a new person who'd never been there and say, 'I want you to meet so-and-so.' And then Irene would sit them down and kind of give them the 'Here's what's going on, here's what we do and what we don't do,' and made sure that person knew she was available if they ever had any questions. Then she'd buy them a drink, or a soda if they didn't drink alcohol."

When it came to drawing blood for the tests, Irene gave

Karen access to a private little dressing room that was typically reserved for drag queens preparing for shows. "It was off to the side, so people weren't staring as anyone came in or out, and that helped a lot."

What an awe-inspiring moment. In true American form, with no blueprint to go off in a highly morally charged pandemic, these folks were finding ways to save lives on the fly. The compassion and ingenuity of doing a mini makeover of a drag-queen dressing room into a makeshift medical clinic makes my nonbinary heart swell with pride and admiration.

Karen's testing visits happened on Saturday nights, and whenever she returned with a positive diagnosis of someone, she'd immediately set up an appointment for them at the health department on the following Monday. She was trained in on-the-spot counseling, but she also made sure to have a wide range of resources available at the health department to help HIV+ people. "We'd get them further counseling, doctors' names, and as time went on, we even got an attorney who would help them with Social Security or Medicaid," she said. "Because a lot of them didn't have enough money to afford treatment. Back then the only HIV medicine available was AZT. It was expensive."[7]

The levels of dysfunction between the US government, the CDC, the FDA, not to mention the capitalist monsters of Big Pharma, resulted in a tragedy in which, at the height of a pandemic, the only treatment available was completely out of reach for most people. Words can never give adequate weight to the injustices and loss of life this created.

The Adams County Health Department also provided anonymous contact tracing services, so a newly diagnosed person wouldn't have to deal with the added anxiety of notifying partners if they weren't up to the task themselves. It's nothing short of miraculous that Karen was able to get the equally important job of contact tracing sorted in a time when these services weren't commonplace.

I'd hoped to talk more with Karen about her experiences working with Quincy's LGBTQIA+ community, but when I reached out for a second interview, I was heartbroken to learn that she had passed away. The sadness was visceral after having had the chance to interview someone so important, someone who had shown so much love to people like me at a time when so many others shunned them. Looking over my notes, I had many more questions I knew I'd never get to ask her.

I waited a few months before contacting her husband, John Spring—who happened to have been Quincy's mayor from 2004 to 2012—to offer my condolences and let him know how much I appreciated all she had done. I was also interested in his take on his wife's crucial work, since they were married during that time, and it turns out he helped her in her mission long before he got into politics.

"I remember in the earliest days she and I would drive to St. Louis to get the AIDS Quilt and bring it back," he told me. "Someone would deliver it to a parking lot in St. Louis, and we'd pick it up, and we'd bring it back here to Quincy University and display it there. We'd also hold a candlelight vigil."

This was the first time I'd ever heard that the iconic AIDS Memorial Quilt—such an important part of queer history—had come through Quincy, and I'm happy to know that at least some Quincians knew of it.

I wanted to find out if the work Karen had done had ever affected her emotionally, but it sounded like she dealt with hard times the same way I do—with humor. "She didn't talk too much about it," John said. "If someone was going through a really difficult time period or the disease had advanced considerably, that was hard on her, but she was very straightforward. She didn't hide anything when she was talking to people, and she always seemed able to crack a joke."[8]

Good golly, Miss Molly, as if I couldn't love her more!

Here I didn't even think there were other gay people in Quincy when I was growing up, and turns out not only was there a thriving subculture but also heroic nurses were providing HIV/AIDS education and testing as well as a lionhearted champion in drag saving lives while serving countless gimlets and vodka crans!

WHEN I WAS a teenager, Irene's Cabaret always felt like a fantastical yet bizarre place that I wouldn't ever get to go to. It wasn't the type of situation where you could sneak in underage. I knew it was an off-limits place to me. Considering my bags had been packed to leave Quincy since age eight, I knew I would have to visit in my college era.

After I turned twenty-one, I went to Irene's Cabaret a handful of times when I came home to visit. I don't think I ever met Irene, though it's possible. I wish now that I'd better understood the importance of the space. At the time, it just seemed like a kooky place where people much older than I was were listening to not-Beyoncé, which was kind of a nonstarter for me. While I stand by my musical choices, I wish I'd revered the space and experienced more.

I wish I'd known to appreciate all of those older members of my community. I wish I'd thought to sit down at the bar and listen to their stories. I'll never know the priceless human connections I could have had with these people, but having that crystal-clear hindsight makes me want to spend time with our LGBTQIA+ elders now while I still can.

Whether it was Irene or the bartenders or just the regulars who'd been going there for years, all of them were so brave. They were unafraid to live their true lives, and were sticking their necks out to help people in a place that could be unwelcoming, to put it lightly. It makes that dingy little hole-in-the-wall bar look a lot more beautiful and golden and amazing in the rearview than it did when I was younger.

There's no question that Irene was Quincy's guardian angel of the queer community, and so many other small towns across the US had figureheads like her, people who opened their arms to frightened, closeted people, gave them a home away from home, and fought through the height of the AIDS crisis to help those around them. It breaks my heart that so many of these incredibly special souls have been lost to time, their stories untold.

In Willie/Irene's case, his spirit was so strong that he didn't even let a horrific hate crime in 1984 hold him back or scare him away from town. He was targeted and attacked in his own home, blinded in one eye, and beaten so badly that the local hospital didn't expect him to live. But doctors were able to stabilize him enough to get him to a larger hospital a few hours south, in St. Louis, where he ended up staying for around five or six months, undergoing surgery after surgery. Doctors had to obtain photos in order to try to put his face back together into anything that resembled what he'd looked like before. He was told that he'd suffered brain damage and would likely feel its effects later in life, and in fact he never fully recovered from the attack. When Willie/Irene passed away in 2015, thirty-one years after he'd been beaten, he died from complications due to those same injuries.

The cruelty and viciousness of that attack leave me at a loss for words.

ALL OF THIS hit home during the episode of *Queer Eye* where we returned to Quincy to recognize my beloved former teacher Kathi Dooley. We were welcomed into a gymnasium full of cheering kids and greeted by an administration that was thrilled to have us there. The episode presented my hometown as a safe haven of acceptance.

Which it could be, but what didn't get included in that episode was that some parents refused to let their kids come to school while we were shooting. Or that a local pastor wrote an op-ed condemning our presence. Or that a week after we packed up our cameras and left, a young gay person was jumped and beaten up in a hate crime and didn't feel safe enough to report it.

Learning about this attack brought up all the feelings of hopelessness I'd had growing up, that there is nobody to protect LGBTQIA+ people. For queer victims of violence, reporting an assault to law enforcement can often compound the trauma of the attack itself. If law enforcement fails to protect you, or doesn't believe you, it can embolden the very people who abused or assaulted the queer person in the first place. Which is why so many LGBTQIA+ victims of violence don't report crimes against them. They don't want to make their lives harder than they already are.

It weighs on me heavily that while we were able to shine a more inclusive light on Quincy, young queer people there—and everywhere—are still not safe to be themselves.

Viewers of shows like *Queer Eye* want to see progress and empowered narratives of pride and resilience, but we need to be just as vocal and visible about the reality of ongoing violence. We can acknowledge support while also staying vigilant about the difficult and uncomfortable realities—the ones that are so often and easily edited out of stories about progress.

The town I called home didn't want me to be a part of it when I was young, but there are people still living in Quincy working hard to make sure that isn't the case for the current—and future—generations. Ryan Jude Tanner graduated from my same high school seven years ahead of me and went on to become a famous Broadway producer with two Tony Awards for Best Revival of a Musical under his belt (out of four different nominations, as well as a slew of other fancy awards from places like the Kennedy Center for other productions).

In 2020, he decided to return to Quincy with his husband, Jay Krottinger, to open a restaurant called The Patio, right down the street from where Irene's Cabaret stood. While it's not exactly defined as a "gay restaurant," it's definitely what I'd call a queer space, and Ryan agreed. "From the very beginning we explained to our team, 'We are going to lead with kindness and goodness here so that everyone feels welcome,'" Ryan told me. "'If you are here and have a problem with any of these things, you really need to leave now.' We lost no one."

That welcoming vibe has brought The Patio equally lovely customers. "I'm seeing all these young and older queer men bringing their moms to eat," he said. "And then the moms pat me on the hand and say, 'My son is just like you,' or, 'My son has a friend like you.' That is incredible progress, and it has been so positive."

That's not to say that Quincy still doesn't have a long way to go. "It's become more of a Republican city," Ryan said. "But taking away party politics, the people of Quincy, their understanding of gay people and compassion for them has improved. Every night I make a point when I'm meeting every customer that I always talk about my husband. I think removing those barriers has improved. I know that they are getting better, but it's not gone."

Ryan's early memories of—and later experiences with—Irene's Cabaret are similar to mine in that it seemed like a place to be avoided until we were old enough to truly understand and appreciate its worth in the community. When he was growing up, his family owned a store nearby, and he recalled, "They were very much opposed to and afraid of the queers around the corner. It was really hard for them to understand. And unfortunately, when you drove or walked by Irene's, sometimes you didn't see people that were beaming with light. They were down on their luck. They were having a hard time. They were pushed to the side. I think that as a young kid coming out, it was very scary. As I got older and I could drive, I would go by real slow, but I was always too afraid to get out of the car." I get it. If you were going to live out and queer, especially back then, it was scary to go to a place that was obviously only for queer people, because it put a stationary target on you.

Like me, Ryan finally went into Irene's Cabaret while visiting home over the holidays. "I'll never forget it," he said. "I went in on Christmas Eve 2002, and when I got inside, I was like, *Well, everybody was wrong all along. These are wonderful, beautiful people!*" While Ryan never had any interactions with Irene herself, he understands the importance of the space that she created: "I know that her impact on Quincy is generational and profound."

"Grateful" isn't strong enough of a word to sum up how I feel about the work that Ryan and his husband are doing in Quincy today with The Patio, continuing what Irene began and creating an environment that makes my hometown a better and safer place for LGBTQIA+ folks. I'm in awe of everyone like Ryan doing this kind of hard work in their own hometowns. I'm not sure my nervous system could handle this same kind of on-the-ground job in Quincy. But for Ryan, thankfully, it's a different story: "Every day that we're in that building and every day we're in Quincy, we feel an anthem in our hearts," he said. "We certainly feel like what we are putting into Quincy, we are getting the same back from the people."[9]

*   *   *

Am I surprised that my little Sherlock Holmes investigation of the hidden queer history of my hometown ended up mostly centering around a bar? Pleasantly so. These establishments have always been safe spaces for LGBTQIA+ people and continue to be important places where we can feel welcomed and free from the oppression of hiding who we are. At a gay bar on Christmas, LGBTQIA+ people can meet others in a similar situation and ~~fuck the pain away~~ commiserate over hot toddies while sharing tales of holiday cheer.

I don't think it's an indictment on queer culture that much of our history is enmeshed in bar culture—they're spaces where people, especially in the past, can be themselves after a long day of hiding in the closet—but it's important to recognize that alcoholism and drug use are extremely high in the LGBTQIA+ community. That's why I love that Irene set up a church space above the bar. It takes a special soul to recognize that there were also spiritual needs to be met.

So many LGBTQIA+ people already grow up in hostile environments, and while we're busy just trying to survive day-to-day, it's easy to forget why it's important to connect with our pasts. By looking deeper into those who paved the way, and honoring the work they did, you might learn from the strength of the queer people who came before us, and perhaps find a similar strength in yourself. If you're feeling particularly isolated, it can be a surprising comfort to explore the rich history of queer icons and pioneers. You can obviously find so much information online and in books, but I hope younger people will look deeper on the local level, dig up more unsung local heroes like Irene West, queer activists who did (and are still doing) their work on the ground, person by person, and deserve just as much praise, honor, and remembrance as our community's more visible icons.

In a time and place where being out of the closet meant risking your life, our LGBTQIA+ elders paved the way for a more accepting society, a world where a kid who gets scolded for wearing dresses and tights can go on to sell out shows and be watched by millions of people. I know that what the Irenes of the world did has made my life experience possible. Celebrating LGBTQIA+ history is more than parades; it can also look like learning and reaching out to the LGBTQIA+ elders in your community. Together, we can build a bridge that leads us from the periphery of society to the beautiful center-stage spotlight we've been destined for all along.

CHAPTER 4

OVERCOMING BODY ISSUES AND LEARNING TO LOVE MY GORGEOUS SELF

Or, stop calling me brave! I'm hot!

I never knew I was body positive. I was positively aware I had a body, but one I found unbearably undesirable to myself and, from what I'd been told, definitely to other people. For much of my life, I couldn't find one thing about the way I looked that I enjoyed. It took me decades to accept my body and eventually celebrate it. As someone who is known for practicing self-love, I'm often unintentionally reminded of the double-edged sword of being associated with body positivity. People are constantly saying things to me like "You're so inspiring for wearing those crop tops and taking your shirt off. I could never do that!" Or "I have an average body too! I struggle with confidence, but then I see you and it gives me hope."

Um, ew? Why does it have to be an act of bravery to wear what makes me feel good? Why would someone see this miraculous body that allows me to live my wonderfully best life and call it average? None of our bodies are average, and our desirability shouldn't be related to how the world at large views and labels them.

Sadly, it took me a long time to realize this.

The foundation of my eventual body dysmorphia was established early. Those Bowflex commercials left an imprint on me. If you're not familiar with the machine and its marketing evils, do yourself a favor and watch their circa early '90s ads on YouTube. The Bowflex itself is basically just a tricked-out weight bench, but damn, I hope whatever ad agency landed that account got paid a butt load of money because here we are, more than twenty-five years later, and I'm still talking about the fucking thing.

The first time I saw one of their commercials it stopped me dead in my tracks. What were these strange heart palpitations? Why did I suddenly feel faint? I was just looking at some oiled-up Adonis working himself into a hypertrophic ball of testosterone, nbd. There was a female fitness actress too; maybe she could be my fun imaginary babysitter. I liked her tights! But she didn't give my stomach the same butterfly feels that the oiled-up-to-oblivion man did. It was crush at first sight. When the commercial ended and my desire to hump a pillow went away, a horrifying despair took hold.

Layered on top of my undeniable interest in that perfectly waxed chest and the problems that presented, I looked at my own body and wondered, *Why don't I look like him?*

I mean, it's not like anybody I knew in real life had abs so ripped that I might slice my finger open just by touching those glorious edges. I'd spent time at the YMCA where my dad worked out, and on summer days I basically lived at the pool. I wasn't surrounded by fitness-model bods, but I had come to the realization that when shirts came off, I definitely didn't look like the other boys. I had a belly and extra skin that hung from my chest, but other boys were rail thin, running around the pool deck with buff lifeguards blowing their whistles at them. Any one of those guys could have ordered a Bowflex and whipped themselves up to look like the man on TV in no time. But not me. I felt like a young Chris Farley in *Tommy Boy*, only obsessed with Barbies, figure skating, gymnastics, and beauty pageants.

Because my negative body image and self-esteem issues developed around the same time when I was beginning to understand my sexuality, I became obsessed with the fact that I did not look the same as the other boys at my school, and this just added to the sense of alienation and shame that I already felt from school bullying, the sexual abuse I'd experienced as a child, and stress over being a generally flamboyant kid in a highly conservative cis hetero environment. Living with the constant anxiety of never knowing what insults would be hurled my way on any given day, as well as the fear that any one of my secrets might become public knowledge, all became too much. Around the age of ten, food became my most soothing coping mechanism, and I threw myself into bags of powdered donuts and frozen burritos.

The fact that decades later I can still remember exactly what I was eating during this period, and why, is a clear example of the insidious intersections of self-worth and a pressure to conform to perfect body standards. I can vividly recall the shame of eating a second box of Thin Mint Girl Scout cookies and then chugging water and doing sit-ups (like that was going to do anything, lol), followed by staring down at my tummy, sobbing uncontrollably, and thinking, *Why can't I stop doing this? When will I ever be hot?*

There was such an intense combination of pain and suffering that led to my disordered eating, but nobody could help me unpack all of that at the time because I was too scared to ask for help. Instead, I had to face the reality of my internal struggle at a routine physical at age twelve, when our family doctor told my mom that I was in the 95th percentile for body mass index (BMI)—*eye roll*—and needed to watch my weight because I was considered obese. And I wasn't even a teenager yet.

As I entered my early teenage years, I knew I had to try to lose weight. But it wasn't for any of the medical reasons presented to me by that doctor. The driving force behind my fourteen- and fifteen-year-old brain was: *Who will ever want to date me, much less hold me till the pain goes away, if I'm too big?*

Healthy, right?

The "who" went from an abstract idea of a hunky Bowflex man to a very real representative in the form of Fyodor, my high school crush. Fyodor had an impossibly gorgeous body, and he could eat whatever he wanted with no consequences. His six-foot swimmer's body was serving flawless Adonis vibes, and the whole package shivered me to my queer core. I knew that if I ever had any chance of nabbing him, I had to become a swimmer to get a body that matched his.

Oh, also, after watching the made-for-TV movie *Perfect Body* starring Amy Jo Johnson (aka the Pink Power Ranger) as an Olympic gymnast hopeful who develops an eating disorder, I decided to start throwing up all the food I continued to binge in excess. Because, honey, there weren't enough swim practices to burn off all those cinnamon rolls and white cheese dips.

I developed a method for this madness by setting a rule that I couldn't throw up any of my regular meals, only the junk food that I binged in between breakfast, lunch, and dinner. Further justification came from the fact that at least I wasn't doing it daily, maybe only twice a week when I would "accidentally" devour a family-size box of pizza rolls or four boxes of Girl Scout Tagalongs and shortbread Trefoils.

As the pounds began to come off, I knew that sensible meals and exercise were doing the real work, but since the weight loss happened while I indulged my urge to purge, I convinced myself at the time that it was helping. To reinforce it even more, people started paying attention to my new look, and I loved it.

A few months into my bulimia routine, my brother caught me throwing up. I was puking hard enough to have developed a bloody nose, and he threatened to tell our mom, so I decided it was time to stop. Staring into a toilet full of undigested snacks, blood pouring down my nose, and my brother barging through the door to witness it all shook me up enough to realize I was on the edge of something extremely dangerous, and I didn't want to be there anymore.

So from that moment forward, I decided I just needed to be a workout binger. Again—healthy, right?

Whenever I decided that I'd overeaten after a meal, I'd supplement my already twice-daily swim practices with gymnastics, running, and cigarettes—anything that might control my appetite and/or work off food that I deemed excessive. (Oh yeah, I'd started smoking by then because I'd heard it was an appetite suppressant. Say it with me, one more time: healthy, right?)

I hate admitting this, but I fluctuated within different areas of this same routine for the next sixteen years or so. From adolescence until around the time I hit thirty, that was the body-control universe I inhabited. I always had to give myself some sort of food restriction, or binge eat, or overexercise, all with the intention of keeping my body approvable enough to find someone who would ultimately love me. Or at least fuck me until that perfect person came along.

Body dysmorphic disorder (BDD) and shame run deep in the gay community. Deeper than the pit in my stomach when Aly Raisman fell off the uneven bars in the qualifying round of the 2015 World Gymnastics Championships in Glasgow. Whenever I went on Grindr or SCRUFF to find a date or a hookup, all of the horrible language I'd already heard about fuckability standards was echoed once more in reactions to photographs of my body.

> You're too fat for me.
> Sorry, not into fat guys.
> I'm only into fit guys.

The way I dressed and acted was something I could easily change, even if it pained me, but my body took a lot more work, and all of it was fueled by a chorus of hateful words telling me that I wasn't good enough. I had no desire to simply be healthy and make better decisions so I could live a long and happy life—I was compelled to change by the disgust aimed at me.

I also want to point out that the judgment I faced represents only a white, femme queer's experience before I was HIV+. BIPOC folks often receive worse cruelty in the LGBTQIA+ community, because in addition to the misogynistic attitudes and body dysmorphic culture, racism runs deep. The number of white gay men who freely talk about not being into Black or Asian men is astounding. A culture that evaluates your total worth based on only your physical appearance cannot connect in a way that sees your humanity. It breeds a lot of buttholes but also a lot of insecurity, shame, and rejection.

I'm still not entirely sure what finally clicked inside me that made me stop chasing the idea of a "perfect" body and searching out other men's validation 24/7. I think I'd just finally seen enough eggplants that I became less interested in dick and more interested in how I felt about myself. The consistent emptiness I felt after casual hookups and emotionless sexual encounters left me numb, and I realized that the validation I was seeking was ultimately only going to come from within.

Recognizing that the good things happening in my career were the results of my own determination and drive likely had a lot to do with it. My work life was clearly changing for the better, but emotional work never happens overnight. I certainly tried many times to change my mindset to become more self-loving, with briefly positive results, but any time I slipped into old habits, I was able to forgive myself because I strongly believe in a "three steps forward, five steps back, and seven steps forward" type of existence. It wasn't a light-bulb moment that led me to self-acceptance but a collection of experiences that allowed me to try things a different way.

There was a point in my life when I included the phrase "body positivity" whenever I talked about my evolving feelings of self-love and care, but I now much prefer the relatively newer concept of "body *neutrality*," which strikes down the idea that I always have to equate feeling good about my body to feeling good in general. Body positivity is nice in theory, but it's an unrealistic expectation to constantly uphold because we are all beautifully complicated humans with near-infinite ranges of emotion. Body neutrality allows for a more naturally holistic relationship with these physical vessels we inhabit, and the idea is to focus on what our bodies can do for us, not how they appear. It's okay for me to have days when I wish I looked a little different, so long as I understand that I can also lead a complete, gorgeous, and fulfilling life that coexists with those feelings.

I think one surprising benefit of all of those empty sexual encounters from my past is that they prepared me to finally be in a space in life where my heart and mind were open, willing, and ready to meet my person, and to have the confidence to try for the relationship I'd always wanted. But even now that I'm happily married and feeling well into my journey of healing, I still find myself wanting random validation from gay men and queer people. However, now I can look at it as a natural part of being a person. I try to be curious about those feelings and remain compassionate and gentle with myself whenever the need flares up in a way that doesn't feel aligned with my authentic self.

Usually when that validation need pops up, it's trying to keep myself separated from an unwanted feeling, and now, most of the time, I'm able to respond to that part and say, "I know you want that external sought-after feeling, but I also know I'm enough."

These days the urges feel much less aggressive and frenetic in terms of what that part of me wants to do to get the attention it thinks I want. The specific desires that pop up, like wanting a cute person to send me a torso pic, or having six cookies instead of sixty-five, aren't quite as harmful as my old ones, because the validation I now seek doesn't require hurting myself with food, overexercising, binging, drugs, or sex.

About that last one. I know this essay started out about body image and self-esteem and then we veered pretty quickly into sex, but it's impossible to write about healing from my compulsive eating without acknowledging my healing from sexual compulsivity as well. They are, for me, inextricably linked, and

I know they are for many others as well. Through two trips to inpatient rehab and years of therapy since, I've learned a lot about impulse control, sitting with my unhealthy urges, dysfunctional cycles, and abuse and trauma, and how all of those things interact in my psyche. Particularly, I've learned that impulses and cravings are not absolute commands from the brain that must be satisfied; they just *feel* like they are. Impulses and cravings will eventually abate if I can just sit with them long enough and not identify with the urge. I practice not letting it overtake me to the point where I'd actually do the knee-jerk behavior I'm trying to ride out. Reading countless books and working with multiple therapists to learn how my destructive adult behaviors reflect similar cycles of abuse from my childhood have taught me so much of what I know about how unprocessed early trauma manifests itself in my adult life. Being aware of all of that helps me make better decisions.

But there's a larger picture to explore here. What were *so many* of us exposed to in life that causes us to hate our bodies? Why is it that at such a young age I came to the conclusion that how my body looked would directly influence my ability to feel happy, connected, and loved?

Oh yeah, it's that fucking Bowflex commercial.

Fine, not just the commercial but what it and thousands of other images and messages like it represent. The idea that if you buy this one thing, you will look like these people. You'll be stunning, you'll be happy, you'll be fuckable, all thanks to a handy machine that folds up under your bed when you're done using it for the day. The messaging is everywhere—magazines, television, movie montages—the idea of a quick fix, focused only on the external while ignoring the internal. It took me far too long to figure out that it's all a lie.

In fact, some of my most miserable times in life were when I was at my supposed "sexiest." In 2014, I went through a phase of doing one hour of hot yoga every morning for almost a year. Six days a week, my three daily meals consisted solely of chicken, broccoli, and sweet potatoes. All to get ready for a season premiere trailer for *Gay of Thrones* that had me shirtless on a beach, and I was determined to look smoking hot when that day came.

You know what's not hot? How fucking hungry, grouchy, and unhappy I was for the several months it took for me to get the body I'd thought I'd always wanted. I finally had six-pack abs, and wouldn't you know it, I was no happier than I'd been before. I didn't feel more balanced. I wasn't filled with more joy. The teaser did end up being pretty funny, but the point is that I had to get the body I thought I'd always wanted to be able to finally see the truth: that we are so much more than our bodies.

They are, of course, important. Bodies are sacred; they are our vessel! But to have love or our worth based on how our bodies look is something we don't deserve. No exercise or diet program or workout machine can give you a lasting sense of worth and acceptance, and finding self-acceptance isn't something that just happens, especially if you're starting from a place of trauma. It means working every single day to reject the negative messages constantly hurled our way by advertising and social media, the insidious missives we internalize, sometimes without even noticing that it's happening.

Even the positive messages we get can morph into tiny blows to our self-esteem. Like I said earlier, I get a lot of messages and comments that are basically slightly different versions of "You're so brave. How do I get the same kind of confidence?" I know the people who send them mean well, and I'm honored that they feel comfortable reaching out to me. But those messages come across as unintentionally cruel. They make me feel like I *shouldn't* feel confident or proud of my body exactly the way it is. Those messages subtly—and I hope, again, unintentionally—reinforce the idea that posting images of anything that isn't an Adonis body ready to win first prize at a fitness competition is a risky proposition.

I believe that in order for all of us to cultivate more body neutrality we need to actively reject the falsehoods inherent in diet and fitness culture. Trust me—you will not be happier or feel more whole if you have visible abs. Fitness companies make their money off creating a mindset of you being just one purchase away from your perfect body, which will bring you the perfect life. Instead, let's practice emotional and mental fitness, because not being judgmental of our bodies and the bodies around us is the real key to body neutrality, and to a happier life. Think about it. We are all beautiful creatures who, against all statistical odds, have arrived here on Earth as the unique individuals we are. You made it here, out of billions of DNA combinations that could've created any person and instead created you, created me, created us.

Your chance to be alive, to chase your dreams, to find your joy, and to pursue your passions is a precious gift. I refuse to waste any more time believing in anything less than my humanity and my right to love and be loved. I know there will still be days when I don't feel this way, but in those moments, I will also know it's because I absorbed some toxic ideas in my past that I'm still unlearning. I've promised myself that every time those feelings come up, I will try to make myself release them back into the past. And I hope you choose to do the same, you stunning fucking queen.

CHAPTER 5

THE DEVIL'S LETTUCE

Or, why is cannabis so vilified, for feck sake?

According to the 1999 iteration of D.A.R.E., the drug prevention program that I (and over one hundred million other US school kids) was forced to take in public school, smoking weed would turn me into an addict plagued by heroin and crack cocaine, and I'd be destined to die a violent and horrible death.

Back then, marijuana was illegal in all fifty states. Now pot is experiencing a meteoric rise to mainstream acceptance across the country. As of this writing, it's recreationally legal in eighteen states as well as the District of Columbia, and legal for medical use in thirty-six states. Even D.A.R.E. has amended its stance, saying that it's "neither safe nor healthy for students and all children under the age of 18 to use marijuana."[1] We love a healthy boundary for developing minds! As well as an evolution away from their false, fear-mongering *Reefer Madness* for kids propaganda.

Besides, D.A.R.E.'s early scare-tactic programming had the opposite intended effect. All it did was make weed seem like that sexy bad boy whose convertible I was desperate to get into. And whenever I stumbled on older kids smoking it, they also made it seem so cool. Overall, enough of a fuss was made about the devil's lettuce that from a pretty young age I'd decided it was something I must try for myself.

I got my first chance at a big family reunion/anniversary party when I was a tween and saw some older kids in the parking lot. I approached them, asked to try it, and to my shock they said yes. I didn't feel much of anything other than super cool for being invited into the circle of smokers. But soon after, I became terrified that my parents might find out and fearful that I was now doomed to a life of drug addiction. (Hmm . . . in retrospect, that sounds like paranoia so maybe I was feeling it.) It took years for me to get up the nerve to try it again with some friends, and that time, I discovered why so many people loved it. It made me feel calm and most everything was much funnier. I was into it.

My relationship to cannabis has evolved a lot over the years, from those innocent childhood experiments to a dependency so deep that it was part of why I went to rehab, in addition to my sexual compulsivity. In my mid- to late twenties I learned to shift away from using weed as a numbing tool and instead began microdosing as a method of self-soothing, which has kept anxiety and depression from creeping in and causing me to relapse on much harder and more dangerous drugs. In short, cannabis has helped me stay stable, and we love her for that.

I know that it's hardly healthy to light something on fire and suck it into your lungs, but weed is far less addictive and much less harmful to your overall health than alcohol, cocaine, meth, and opioids. Not that we'd know this from scientific studies in the US. Since marijuana is categorized as a Schedule 1 illegal substance, the United States government has never funded research to discover its potential for medical benefits. We have to rely on international and privately funded studies to understand how it can help with issues like chronic pain, irritable bowel syndrome, epilepsy, Parkinson's disease, post-traumatic stress disorder, and easing the withdrawal symptoms of harder drugs like opiates and methamphetamines.

I've used cannabis for both healing and fun purposes for almost a decade now, but in many states where cannabis is not legal for recreational use, like Arkansas, Mississippi, Idaho, and North Dakota, it's an automatic federal felony for anyone to be in possession of it or the paraphernalia used to administer it. Which means that if someone has a small amount on them for personal use and gets caught in a state where it's illegal, they can be charged incredibly steep felony fines and face incarceration.

Under United States Civil Asset Forfeiture laws, if law enforcement even suspects that you may be involved in criminal activity, like, say, drug trafficking (and by trafficking, I mean carrying a couple of joints across a state line), they're allowed to take any possessions they believe were involved in the illegal activity. That includes your car if you were driving and got pulled over. It can take years of expensive legal challenges to ever get your belongings back, regardless of whether you even end up being convicted of the crime you're charged with.

Cannabis use can be held against parents in custody battles, and it can be used against people to tie them to completely unrelated crimes. If you end up being incarcerated, it can cause permanent financial ruin and family separation. Maybe D.A.R.E. was right in a way: weed can ruin your life—if you get busted. But unlike so many of my fellow pot smokers, I've never experienced any legal ramifications from my cannabis use. Why is that? You've got one guess and it rhymes with "bright frivilege."

One of the first times I saw white privilege in action (but at least a full decade before I ever even heard the phrase) was during my Christmas break back home from college. It was Christmas Eve, and two of my (white) girlfriends and I wanted to smoke a festive holiday joint and have a celebratory "All I Want for Christmas Is You" Mariah moment.

We called around to our former weed hookups to see who had some to sell, and while waiting to hear back we aimlessly drove around town and hit up a McDonald's drive-through. Naturally, I needed an apple pie to help pass the time and pre-game my munchies.

At one point, a police officer pulled up right next to us and gave us the stink eye but then drove away. We continued to cruise across town, and another police car rolled up alongside us at a stoplight, looked us up and down, and then sped off. Right after this second law enforcement encounter our friend called us back to say that he'd gotten our weed and that we should come by to pick it up. We got the goods and started to drive back to my friend's house, where we all planned to spend the night so no one would be behind the wheel while stoned. Safety first!

After driving a couple of blocks, a police car snuck up and pulled us over. We were terrified as the officers approached, the red and blue flashing lights making everything seem surreal and amping up our anxiety. I was the one with the pot on me, so I quickly shoved it down my pants and nestled it securely against my taint.

After asking to see all of our IDs, the cops only ordered my two friends to get out of the car. I'm not sure if it was because they saw that I was under eighteen or if they recognized my last name and knew who my grandpa was (he is an extremely well-known person in our hometown), but I breathed a sigh of relief.

I also knew I didn't have to worry about my friends, because they knew exactly what to say and how to say it. "No, you can't search my car without a warrant," one snapped. "I want to call my mom and dad so they can call our lawyer."

The cops separated the two of them for questioning about what we'd been up to all night, and once their stories matched up—that we'd just been catching up while home for the holidays and had gone to McDonald's—they let us go. I couldn't believe our luck, but looking back at that night now, I can clearly see that luck had nothing to do with it.

One month later, while I was back at college, those same two girls were hanging out with two other friends, all of them relaxing with a joint indoors, when a neighbor called the cops. She told them that she'd seen two Black men enter her building and that a strong odor of marijuana was now coming from the apartment they'd gone into. Because of that call, the cops were able to immediately obtain a search warrant, and all of them were violently thrown to the floor when the police raided the place. The weed was confiscated, and each of them was served with felony charges.

Let's recap. A car of white kids, including the progeny of

a respected local business owner, were let go by the cops after they were unable to come up with a valid reason for a search. But when two of those same kids were with Black friends inside a private residence, there was no chance of escape for any of them. The felony charges against the two white girls were dropped, but the ones against the two Black men were ruinous. They couldn't afford the thousands of dollars it would have cost to hire an attorney skilled enough to help them get less harsh sentences, and instead they had to opt for an overworked and underpaid public defender. A single afternoon of relaxing with a joint resulted in jail time in addition to thousands of dollars in legal fees. Who knows how many opportunities were lost to those two young men because of a single racially motivated phone call?

To easily understand how we got to this point, all you need to do is watch Ava DuVernay's brilliant documentary *13th*, which should be required viewing in every school in the United States, as well as for anyone thinking of running for public office. She and her team of brilliant researchers and interview subjects put together a devastating record that encapsulates over 150 years of history in a potent, straightforward way.

The film shows how the Thirteenth Amendment of the Constitution, which outlawed slavery, contains a loophole that allows for slavery as punishment for a crime, which essentially created a system that immediately served to enslave Black people once more, but this time within prisons. It was a deliberate move to keep white supremacy in place, and that loophole contributes to the US incarcerating nearly 25 percent of the entire world's prisoners, despite having only 5 percent of the world's population. In other words, one out of four incarcerated people on the entire planet are locked up in our country, and one out of five of those are in for a drug offense, and many more for minor misdemeanors.

Both the Pew Research Center and the NAACP report that the Black imprisonment rate is more than five times that of whites, and once you've been in prison, you're a felon, which comes with severe voting restrictions, and some states are lobbying to take away a felon's right to vote entirely.[2] Organizations like the American Civil Liberties Union are working to overturn felony disenfranchisement, but as of now there are only two states that allow all of their residents to vote: Maine and Vermont. Eliminating the right to vote of many Black Americans has been a conscious goal to keep white supremacy in power.

Marijuana possession is one of many things considered "minor crimes" Black Americans can be convicted of and put in prison for. There are several reasons why this particular "crime" has had a hugely significant historical impact. Please keep in mind that entire books and PhD dissertations are written on this subject, and I have a fairly limited word count, so consider all of the information I'm about to unload on you as a

Gay of Thrones-speed recap with nothing funny about it at all.

One large issue with hemp back in the day had nothing to do with smoking buds. The plant itself, with its strong and versatile fibers, was a big threat to the cotton industry, so agriculturally, there were big business forces working to keep it from becoming a popular crop.

Pot was approved for a few medicinal purposes starting around 1850, and while some states had their own laws against personal use, things got way worse in the 1930s. After Prohibition ended, federal agents needed something new to go after, and that's when this nightmare named Harry J. Anslinger began his rise to power as the first commissioner of the Federal Bureau of Narcotics. His racist agenda laid out all of the drug law foundations that Nixon would later use to kick off the War on Drugs.

Harry was a noted racist, even for his time period. (A racist's racist, if you will.) Recreational marijuana use wasn't all that widespread in the US; it was mostly found along the Mexican border and in jazz clubs. Guess what Harry hated more than anything, though? Quite literally, Black and Brown people, and especially jazz! He began a vicious smear campaign against pot, and referred to it as "marijuana" or "marihuana" rather than "cannabis," the more commonly used term at the time, in order to make it appear more Mexican, and therefore scary, to whites. He also made sure that plenty of people across the US saw the word "marijuana" written out in print by partnering with Hearst newspapers for a blitz of articles now called the "Gore File." They were essentially lurid tales of axe murders and rapes all caused by Black and Brown people under the influence of marijuana. It was a concerted effort to plant a false racist ideology linking cannabis to horrific violence being carried out on white folks by people of color. This should shock your ass. It means the generations who raised us were indoctrinated with these racist false narratives around cannabis.

Hideous Harry understood the power of framing a narrative. And he tried to stop others from developing their own: he targeted Billie Holiday especially hard because of her song "Strange Fruit," since it was a rallying cry against lynching. His Federal Bureau of Narcotics agents made her life a living hell with their constant harassment and even planting drugs during periods when she was actually clean and sober, right up until her literal dying day. Meanwhile, another celebrity with a widely known drug problem, Judy Garland, escaped all of his wrath due to the color of her skin. His hatred of drugs was racially motivated, plain and simple.

All of the work he did to criminalize and demonize cannabis set the stage for Richard Nixon's establishment of the Drug Enforcement Administration (DEA) in 1973. Pot, along with heroin, had already been made a Schedule I drug with the Controlled Substances Act of 1970, which carried the highest penalties for possession. Want to know why? I'll let this transcript of a recording of Richard Nixon advisor John Ehrlichman explain. (Thanks again to Ava and *13th* for this revelation.)

> *The Nixon campaign in 1968, and the Nixon White House after that, had two enemies: the antiwar left and black people. You understand what I'm saying? We couldn't make it illegal to either be against the war or black, but by getting the public to associate the hippies with marijuana and blacks with heroin, and then criminalizing both heavily, we could disrupt those communities. We could arrest their leaders, raid their homes, break up their meetings, and vilify them night after night on the evening news. Did we know we were lying about the drugs? Of course we did.*[3]

I can't even make a figure skating joke here because that transcript is so brutal.

Remember how the world was so horrified when images went viral of federal agents ripping children from the arms of their parents on orders from the Trump administration? Well, we've been separating children from parents and destroying families in America for hundreds of years, starting with the colonization of this country and the decimation of its Indigenous peoples, followed by chattel slavery, and followed again by the laws passed that targeted Black and Brown, and, while we're at it, LGBTQIA+, Americans, ensnaring them in what would grow to become our mass incarceration system. Things grew even worse when Nixon wanted to get reelected but was scared of white liberals and Black people. So he created the DEA, cementing marijuana as a Schedule 1 drug, meaning it had no medical benefits and had a high potential for abuse, so its possession was a felony, whereas cocaine, which was seen more as a rich white-collar drug, was classified as a Schedule 2, so its possession was a misdemeanor.

Reagan upped the ante with the War on Drugs in the 1980s, and the incarceration rates within Black communities exploded even higher due to crack cocaine. It's yet another example of justice for all clearly being justice only for a certain few. Racism, power, human suffering, and voter suppression were the tent poles of that injustice. It's crystal clear that state and federal governments have the power to target specific communities and take away their agency with laws designed to keep them down.

Thankfully our country's relationship to cannabis has come a long way, but not nearly far enough. As of this writing, President Biden has called for its decriminalization on a federal level, which is a great start. But the incarceration that separated parents from their kids, the endless debt from legal fees, and the lasting felony charges on personal records have ruined lives, the staggering majority of which are Black and Brown families. Nothing short of the full-blown legalization of cannabis and the expungement of all cannabis-related offenses is enough.

Actually, that's only the beginning. I think people who have historically paid the heaviest price for marijuana laws should be the ones who stand to benefit the most from its legalization. Just look at the prosperity cannabis legalization has created in the state of Colorado. They crossed the one-*billion*-dollar revenue mark in 2019. When it comes to handing out new business licenses, grants, and loans, it should be Black and Brown people first, followed by anyone living in poverty. Are you with me? I want everyone to wake up and get activated about cannabis legalization and reparative racial justice because it's a real opportunity for this country to give something back to the communities who've paid such a high price for everyone else's privilege and abundance. Including my own.

Speaking of, I am an unapologetic pot user but should probably also address that I'm a tenacious queen who has been to rehab twice for sexual compulsivity with a side of marijuana dependence. Both times I came out, my intention was to stay sober from all mind-altering substances. Did I succeed? No. After each of my rehab stints, I managed to remain weedless for no more than two months. And both times that I caved, I felt really disappointed in myself. But after the second time, I realized that maybe the problem isn't that I smoke every day but that I *think* it's a problem I smoke every day.

Make all the stoner-logic jokes you want. I can take them, because I'm focused on self-care and harm reduction. I have no shame saying that I am dependent on marijuana, because using it has allowed me to recover from my truly destructive addictions, as well as depression, and I can honestly say that my life is better now than it ever has been. If smoking a joint means I'm not doing meth and seeking validation through sex, then I say it's working for me! Sobriety isn't a one-size-fits-all thing, and part of harm reduction is understanding that each person has their own healing journey that works best for them.

D.A.R.E. taught me that pot would be a gateway drug to harder substances like cocaine, meth, ecstasy, and crack, and while it's true that I tried pot before I dabbled in any other drugs, I don't think pot was what caused me to start experimenting. Considering I can barely walk past a new Pop-Tarts flavor in the store and not rip the box open right then and there, it's safe to say my impulse control is not the highest and I likely would've tried harder drugs regardless. Cannabis did not throw me off my life's track, but I know that it played a huge role in getting me back on it.

At one point in my life, right after my stepfather passed away, I was still relapsing on meth with regularity while also abstaining from weed. I was miserable, so I went on antidepressants, but my body never reacted well to any of the ones I tried. Which is normal—everyone's body chemistry is different, and just because the meds didn't work well for me doesn't mean they don't work miracles for others. I know plenty of people whose lives have been turned around for the better by antidepressants. For whatever reason, though, my own brain wasn't having them. Some even made me feel worse and act out even more.

When I turned back to pot, I discovered that even it couldn't make me feel good anymore. Whenever I smoked, I just became paranoid and edgier than Moira Kelly's character in *The Cutting Edge*. There was a reason for this, though.

In case you're not familiar, there are three different kinds of cannabis: *sativa*, *indica*, and hybrids, which are essentially combinations of *sativa* and *indica* achieved through intentional plant breeding, and basically all pot you find now is from a hybrid plant. (If you are familiar with all of this and rolling your eyes at me right now for stating the obvious, feel free to skip the next two paragraphs.)

Broadly defined, *sativa* is known to produce a more cerebral and giggly kind of high—energizing and good for creativity. This is the type you'd want if you felt like cleaning your house or writing a song or being social or living in a dancing-movie-montage moment. *Indica* produces more of a body high, a feeling of relaxation from the neck down, and it's commonly associated with a more mellow stoned feeling. Frat boys getting their lungs smoky for the first time tend to remember the difference between the two by calling this one "in-da-couch."

Hybrids are crossbred combinations of the *sativa* and *indica* varieties that can provide a more customized feeling, and there are endless combinations with something for everyone of legal age. Feel like confidently telling your cancer to fuck off while getting your appetite back and giggling uncontrollably at the word "schnitzel"? There's a hybrid for that. Want a relaxing body high that will also keep your brain invested in the plot of a German expressionist film on The Criterion Channel? Someone's got you covered. Just like with antidepressants, though, it's important to remember that everyone's chemical makeup is different, and sometimes it can take a while to find a strain that feels right for you. If pot is even right for you to begin with, which it might not be!

Up until my post-rehab life, I was a diehard *sativa* slut whose only goal when I smoked was to get rip-roaringly high. But after doing so much work on myself, that wasn't what I wanted anymore, especially because I'd also acquired a newfound freaked-out state whenever I smoked. Then I started to hear about people using cannabis as medicine and microdosing it. This definitely felt like a gray area of recovery, and it made me uncomfortable due to all of my internalized D.A.R.E. fears, but at that point in my life I was willing to try anything. Nothing else was working, so I decided to give it a shot and headed to a weed dispensary in Venice for a chat with one of their very knowledgeable "budtenders."

I opened up to her about all of the anxiety and paranoia that now accompanied my *sativa* use, and she started asking me some questions. Are you a morning person? Yes! Are you naturally creative? *Yes!* Are you pretty high energy? *Yassss, queeeeeeen!*

Based on my answers, she suggested that *sativa* might not be the best strain for my natural disposition. "For someone like you with a lot of energy already, you may not need to rev your engines like that," she explained. "An *indica* might help bring you into balance."

I've always had an all-or-nothing mentality, and I'd defi- nitely been ripping full bong hits of *sativa* each time I tried smoking again, so it made sense that that's what was bringing me to anxiety tears. I took her advice and began experimenting with my intake, always in small doses. I switched to *indica* and would nibble a bit of a cannabis gummy or just take a quick puff of a joint to give me the bit of relaxation I needed while keeping my debilitating sadness and meth cravings at bay.

It was a healing time of exploring my relationship with cannabis, and I ultimately discovered that it allowed me to live a stable and happy life. I still have my down days and worries like anyone else and I try to fully process them, so this is not an escapist route by any means. Okay, fine, it is a tiny bit escapist, but not so much that my world is burning down around me. As one of my favorite drag queens from college told me, every girl has her hobby. There are certain things that have gotten all of us through the hellish last few years, so you pick your poison, whether it's Animal Crossing, Peloton workouts, or pie, and do what you need to do.

I also need to reiterate (what is it, the fourth time now?) that this is just my personal experience. You might be thinking *Why so defensive about this, hun?* It's because people have such rigid and judgmental ideas of what healing should look like for other people—and that kind of shaming approach does absolutely nothing to help addicts. It's a mindset that just helps other people gloat and feel holier-than-thou. But like Buddha says, there are endless routes to the top of the mountain, and my particular harm-reduction/relaxation model won't work for everyone. For many, a fully sober approach is the best path to recovery. Who knows? Maybe someday I'll do that too, but it's not what works for me at this point in my life. In the trauma and wreckage of depression and addiction, a person deserves to have every tool at their disposal to live a productive life, one that's happy and free of self-harming behaviors.

We know now that the stigmas attached to cannabis use are based in racism, fearmongering, and policy designed to keep white supremacy in power. Once we move past our outdated notions about the dangers of some beautiful buds, who knows how we can harness the power of the plant for healing and re-covery? Our country's racist history of cannabis prohibition has drastically prevented us from even scratching the surface of the multitude of benefits marijuana might have. Potentially, it has the power to save lives.

In January 2021, the Centers for Disease Control and Pre-vention reported that more than 95,000 Americans on average die each year due to excessive alcohol use. That's 261 deaths a day.[4] You know how many are attributed to marijuana? None.[5]

Considering the role that cannabis has played in my heal-ing journey, I feel it should be legally available to everyone over eighteen, and federal funds must be allocated to discover even more positive properties of cannabis. CBD just scratches the surface, as I learned after interviewing Jeff Chen, the hunky founder and executive director of the UCLA Cannabis Research Initiative. THC (the psychoactive element of mari-juana) and CBD (a nonpsychoactive chemical compound in the plant that you've no doubt seen in everything from shampoo to granola bars) are just 2 of 120 cannabinoids in the plant to be explored. One that Jeff is particularly excited about is called THCV, which in some studies has been shown to curb appetite and improve blood-sugar levels of diabetics. What else is hiding in that beautiful leafy bounty? There's a whole garden of healing secrets if we could just get out of our own way and actually study it!

I'll get off my cannabis-infused soapbox now, but let me finish by saying that the war unfairly waged on weed is nothing short of a war on people, and it must end. Folks have suffered long enough. And if this essay has upset you in any way, try smoking a joint to calm down. (But only if you can do so legally and safely!) Regardless of whether you partake or not, make sure to vote in all of your local-level elections, not just the big ones, so we can finally rid our country of the insidious monsters responsible for keeping our problematic pot laws unchanged. Vote. Those. Fuckers. Out. And until then, aim high.

CHAPTER 6

A LOVE LETTER TO HAIRDRESSING

Or, trust me, you do not want your hairstylist
to dread having an appointment with you

I love people, I love to do hair, and I love being behind the chair.

Ew, now I feel like Miranda in the *Sex and the City* episode when she's overconfident on the couch with the guy from her gym and then he ghosts her. The point is, I spent twelve years of my life doing people's hair full-time— constantly refining techniques, building meaningful connections with my clients, and developing my marketing and business skills. Combined, all of those different elements from my original career choice taught me so many lessons, and even though I'm no longer in the salon full-time, I still use all of the knowledge I gained there in practical situations every day.

I'll never fall out of love with the craft. I lose hours watching genius hair cutting, coloring, and styling tutorials on YouTube, TikTok, and Instagram, and love nothing more than giving my friends spontaneous haircuts and turning into a kitchen beautician for my mom.

But if I ever meet you in person, don't get nervous that I'm obsessing over how your hair looks. When I'm talking to someone, I try to focus on face and words first—I refuse to be distracted by bulk or asymmetry or brassy hues or inky hairlines . . . Okay fine, sometimes I do notice if it's really bad, but I swear that I'm noticing your humanity first and questionable hair decisions second. After all these years I hope I never stop observing all the ways I *could* change someone's hair, because it's so fun to fantasize about how I would approach the process! Coloring hair is an intoxicatingly creative skill. It mixes art, science, and technique with different personalities, and to this day the process fills me with joy and wonder. And sure, I know how to correct a brassy blond into a more ashy shade or fix a shag gone mullet, but the most important lessons I've learned working with hair have nothing to do with cut or color.

The first salon I worked at, in Scottsdale, Arizona, is where I learned about self-sufficiency, discovered success, found independence, and was able to take responsibility for being relied on by others. After completing a brief apprenticeship program, I worked hard to stay busy with clients of my own, and if I showed up at work and saw that I didn't have any appointments scheduled in my book, I'd go to the mall with business cards and offer free haircuts and blowouts just to be able to practice and continue learning as much as I could—to keep my hands busy and hopefully build a thriving clientele of my own in the process. I wasn't going to sit in the back room of the salon and wait for walk-ins. The alternative to being successful in this self-employed rental salon, or any salon for that matter, was moving home to Quincy, which was a chance I wasn't willing to take. I knew relying on walk-in clients would take time I didn't have. I needed to build up regular clients with a quickness to make it in the world and to accomplish my other main goal in my twenties: to not need to ask my parents or family for money ever again. My determination matched that of Evgenia Medvedeva during the 2019 World Figure Skating Championships, holding on to her last double axel against all odds, and with an injury, to secure her (at the moment) last World medal, which was a lovely bronze.

That go-getter drive didn't always serve me so well, though. There's one particular client from that early period I'll never forget. I'd only had one job the entire day—a thirty-dollar blow-dry. Considering I'd started at 10 a.m. and the clock was pushing 6:30, I'd averaged about $2.50 an hour after taxes. I was in the middle of some mental math about how many packets of Pop-Tarts and frozen pizza I'd be able to afford for the week when I heard the familiar ring of the bell above the salon's door, indicating a client had just walked in. I didn't recognize the woman from my spot in the back room, where I tried to examine her on the security camera. I knew no one else had another appointment scheduled for the evening, and I was the only one hungry enough to stay late for a new client. I was about to jump up from my seat and claim her when I did a double take at the monitor screen.

The woman had straight, waist-length hair, which immediately made me pause. Even with only about two months of experience under my belt at that point, I knew the probability was high that an issue would arise if this client wanted anything other than a blow-dry. Not that I like to indulge in stereotypes, but if someone walks into a salon with a one-length haircut that reaches down to their butt and they aren't under the age of six, there's a very good chance you'll end up with a control-obsessed nightmare human on your hands.

My eager young self was undeterred, so I shimmied up to the front desk to see what she'd come in for. She seemed to be somewhere in her forties, and her overall hair color was a beautiful light brown. From the side of her head that was facing me I noticed a bit of gray that suited her well.

"Hello, how are you? I'm Jonathan. How can I help this evening?"

"W-well," she stammered, "I saw a commercial for an at-home highlights box kit and thought I'd give it a go, but . . ."

She turned so I could finally see the right side of her head. Picture, if you will, long, Cher-like hair with a center part, but on only one side of her head there is an orangey red circle about the size of a coaster on the outermost layer of hair. There was also a trapezoid-ish shape on the back crown of her head and what appeared to be a splotchy gigantic triangle shape behind her ear. My eyes ceased communicating with each other as one wandered northeast and the other southwest, skittering all over the kaleidoscope shapes of sunset colors. She explained that after she'd purchased the kit she assumed all she had to do was mix up the color and paint random shapes onto her hair, but for some reason that she didn't get into, only on one side of her head. And split evenly down the middle.

Putting aside that she'd thought adding circles, triangles, and squares was the right way to go, the highlighting kit she'd used wasn't even bleach. It's what is called a high lift tint, meant to be applied to naturally light hair to make it very blond, but if applied to dark hair turns out blaringly red, red-orange, or just orange. In short, a corrective color mayhem. Definitely not the creamy blond tone promised on the box.

She explained that she was extremely averse to haircuts, which I'd already clocked from looking at her on the security camera. Had she cut it even once in the past three years? No. Did it look like mice had been chewing on the ends that reached her belt? Yes.

She was at least cognizant enough to realize that her kitchen beautician coloring job was a disaster, but after all she'd put herself through, she still wanted highlights, just ones that were lighter and more uniform. An older and more experienced colorist (or maybe just an older and more experienced *me*) would've said, "Honey, even if you handed me a million dollars and told me we could travel back in time and prevent Michelle Kwan from being injured just before the 2006 Torino games and make sure she won the gold medal—with no negative butterfly-effect consequences—you would never convince me to start this color correction at 6:30 p.m. on a new client. Either we go all-over brown or no dice."

Actually, *maybe* if she could have made Michelle get that gold medal I'd consider it, but I'd need at least a day or two to think, and to call Michelle and see how much it's worth to her at this point.

And yet the situation before me felt familiar. For some reason, highlight hellscapes and color-correction nightmares have always gravitated towards my chair. Maybe it's because the hair gods know I love a massive project. In any case, I agreed to take her on and spent the next four hours working on this woman's DIY disaster. After wrapping the proper areas in foil with the various color fixes I mixed up, I painstakingly highlighted her entire head, painting it a lovely brown in between the foil sections. After two rounds of toning the highlights into natural-looking, subtle sun-kissed streaks, followed by a tiny trim to get rid of the split ends and a blowout, the front desk person was long gone. It was just me and this new client alone in the salon at 11:30 p.m., and she looked stunning after a long evening of hard work.

I'd told her before we began that I charge $50 an hour for corrective color. Since I was feeling giddy with success, I told her that the blow-dry was on me, so her total came to $250 even. She handed me her credit card and I swiped it.

Declined.

Looking desperate, she asked me to try it again, so I did. Still declined. Two different cards later, her tears started to flow. "I can bring you a check," she stammered. "I will pay you somehow. I don't know what could have happened. I'll be back, I promise!"

At that moment, I realized I'd been completely bamboozled, and I was never getting paid for the incredible work I'd just done. I was too exhausted to fight, so I sighed and told her not to worry about it, that it had been my pleasure to help. She said her ride was arriving soon, so I opened the door and locked it behind her after she left. I cleaned up my station, washed out my color bowls, and packed up for the night, feeling defeated but also proud that I had known how to fix something so daunting.

I left via the backdoor, and as I drove out of the parking lot, through the alley and back around to the front of the salon, I saw the woman standing alone, just off to the side of the entrance, her now-beautiful hair blowing in the wind, illuminated by the streetlight she stood under. I slowed down to admire my work, then pulled over and rolled down the window.

"Are you okay?"

"My ride, um, isn't coming." She had a hard time making eye contact and seemed embarrassed.

All of a sudden it hit me that this woman was going through something much bigger than her reckless at-home highlight. I was only nineteen years old and didn't know any better, so I offered to give her a ride home. I turned on Leona Lewis and followed the woman's directions to her house. We didn't speak much, and I prayed she wasn't going to shank me with a pen from her purse and throw me out the window. I was keenly aware this was how an episode of *Unsolved Mysteries* would start, but I also wanted to do the right thing.

We made it to her place twenty minutes later. She got out of the car, thanked me for my time, and went inside.

I was happy that I hadn't been robbed and murdered, but

since colorists have to pay for their own supplies, I'd quite literally paid out of pocket to fix her hair. Instead of getting angry or upset, I wondered if there was a lesson to be learned from the whole experience, aside from *Don't take on mysterious messes right before clocking out for the day.*

Ultimately, I ended up feeling grateful. She'd given me a taste of what not setting boundaries looks like. She also taught me I could fix a gnarly color. I'd gotten to practice my skills and correct one of the most botched hair-color experiments gone wrong I'd ever seen. Even though I hadn't been entirely sure how good it would turn out, I created work I knew I could now be proud of. Bonus: I wasn't murdered in the process of taking a stranger home after her appointment! As the hairdresser half of that one-night stand, those were my big takeaways.

But for you, as a salon client, the lesson I hope you'll take from this tale is different.

Let me break it down for you: Around 95 percent of hairdressers are not paid a fee for working out of a salon. (Don't hold me to that exact number, but it's a very educated estimate.) There's no guaranteed minimum wage, many salon owners skirt the Fair Labor Standards Act since we work as independent contractors, and for stylists and colorists in particular, the overhead is huge since we're responsible for supplying and paying for all of our own materials. The color itself—whether you're doing someone's roots or a massive transformation—can get expensive. So when a client cancels without notice, we typically can't call someone else in on the fly to take that spot. Even when we have a waiting list in case of cancellations, the time you booked might not fit with someone else's since every job is different. One person's hair might take two hours and another's might take six. Sometimes more. The time your appointment has been booked for has a very specific reason behind it and canceling last-minute can affect the rest of the day.

Even running late can cause a domino effect through the entire salon. Considering I was always a tiny bit late for my first appointment of the day, I'm the last one to talk, but I would always (well, most of the time) be able to catch up.

What most people don't take into consideration is that hairdressers aren't just service providers. We're artists. We take a lot of time, money, and care to provide a safe, clean, engaging, fully equipped salon space, and too many clients take that for granted. Sometimes safety comes in the form of protecting you from salon culture or your own impulsive hair instincts. It could be a salon owner pressuring you to do more than what the client needs, or it could be a client asking for more than their hair integrity or daily hairstyling routine can take.

I don't think enough clients realize the level of attention to chemistry, communication, empathy, and pure artistic craftsmanship that goes into what we do. But instead of being treated like the scientist-slash-therapist we are expected to be, we are talked down to and treated as if we work full-time for the person getting their hair done. On the flip side, a little kindness goes a long way.

It's tough to get a business up and running, but developing relationships with clients whose company I cherished (and whom I made look incredible) made all of the work worth it. That's why in my decade-plus of being a hairdresser, I think maybe the hardest thing I've dealt with professionally is breakups—either having to let go of a client myself or realizing that I'd been fired by one of my favorites.

With the latter, I can't recall a time when it happened to my face, but there were several times over the years when a regular client stopped reaching out or never came back. I know that I shouldn't take a client moving on personally—in the same way that many clients don't understand what we're up against, we have no idea what's going on in their private lives except for the stuff they choose to tell us—but being ghosted as someone's stylist naturally leads to hurt feelings. I mean, rejection of any kind sucks for anyone, and for me, it was always especially difficult since I consider myself an artist first. Why didn't you love my work and want to be hair-colorist married to me for eternity? I'd find myself internally playing out Diane Keaton's scream-crying speech in *The First Wives Club* when she discovers her husband is sleeping with her therapist: "I am *sorry* that I allowed myself to love you for all those years. I'm *sorry* I did nothing but be there for you every minute of every day and support you in your every *move*!!" I'M SORRY!

Fine, maybe comparing those moments to Diane's performance is a little overdramatic, but it always felt like the person wasn't turning their back on just my skills and vision but my personality as well. At the end of the day, I have to hold on to the second tenet in *The Four Agreements*, Don Miguel Ruiz's seminal self-help book based on Toltec wisdom: Don't take anything personally.[1] Maybe my client just wanted something different, wanted a change.

If you're a client who's on the fence, like maybe you just started seeing someone new and your color is almost there but not quite right, I think it's good (quite important, actually) to give that person a few more tries before giving them the boot. Due to how slowly hair grows, and the permanent nature of hair color, it can sometimes take multiple layers and applications of color for your hair to fully reach your joint vision. Healthy hair takes commitment, time, patience, and communication with your stylist.

All that said, if you truly feel the relationship has run its course, listen to that. If you value the relationship you developed with your now-former hair person, maybe send them an email or give them a call and say you've really enjoyed your time together, but you're going to another salon. That's a lovely and respectable move, and it will mean a lot to the person you've been working with. I get that breakups are scary, though, so if you'd rather not face it head-on, then fine—run away and don't look back. It's really up to you.

Ghosting is one thing, but over the decade-plus time I spent behind the chair, I've also had several client relationships that dipped into the frenemy pool. For the most part, our conversations would be fun and intimate, and they were always happy with my work, but there were also moments of tension that would flare up. Backhanded compliments or questions about every decision during the application of a hair service. I'm an over-communicator with clients because I want people to feel at ease with the hair-coloring process, especially if it's new to them. But sometimes I'd be in the middle of a friendly, good-natured chat with a client who'd suddenly sit up straight, raise her voice, point a finger at me, and demand, "Why are you doing it like that?"

Or there'd be someone who'd berate an assistant for not rinsing her hair enough (even though it was thoroughly rinsed) or say cruel things about another client in the salon if she believed they were talking too loudly, or didn't like a person's appearance or disposition.

I'd get especially frustrated when a client and I would verbally agree on a price before I began, and then when it came time to pay, they'd start questioning the quality of my work. There were a few people who tried to pull that one—not every time they came in but enough times that I knew to expect it as a possibility. I'd usually try to chalk it up to their own life stress and show grace. Especially when building a new business somewhere, I'd have to find the right balance of what I was willing to tolerate in pursuit of my business's success.

Anyone who has worked in any sort of service industry has had the mantra "The customer is always right" beaten into their brain. But I'm here to tell you, *"Not always."* One client in particular comes to mind (let's call her Svetlana). I'd done her hair for close to half a decade before things fell apart for good. I'd always enjoyed working with her, even though she'd sometimes give me a hard time to varying degrees, in all the ways I just outlined and more. Everything would be fine and then *bam*: she would make a loud, rude comment to my assistant or complain about why something was taking so long with so much irritation in her voice that it caused a scene, even in an already noisy and packed salon.

But again, grace. I'm fully aware of my own capacity to get testy and say things in a tone or way that I don't really mean, so I always wanted to give Svetlana the benefit of the doubt, since in every other way I considered her a friend as well as a client. In the early days of *Queer Eye*, I'd return to Los Angeles every weekend to maintain my clients since I had no idea if the show would be successful or not. It was very important to me to keep up those relationships. As my client load increased, Svetlana's continued cancellations, with no notice and refusals to pay my cancellation fee, as well as her unnecessarily rude remarks to my assistant and myself became more and more intolerable.

Eventually I told her that I'd no longer be able to do her hair. I had put up with her varying degrees of nastiness because she'd stayed loyal to me during the years I was in and out of rehab and struggling to make it, and at some point along the way I'd even become convinced that I deserved her mean treatment. I finally realized that she was more loyal to the idea of treating me badly than she was to my art. For that, she summarily had to be fired. I knew I was a caring, hardworking stylist who liked to make clients happy, and if a client can't respect my work, it's not my job to comfort them while they take advantage of me.

I think about Svetlana sometimes, though, and miss the good parts of our relationship. She could be problematic, but she was also kind and caring at times—she knew all about my family and always asked about them, and we had a whole catalog of inside jokes. I know that when she acted like a total nightmare, it wasn't necessarily about me. The frustration she had with other people at the salon, with her friends and family, all accumulated to create the relationship she had with me, but at some point I outgrew her energy and chose to create space for new energy in my life and clientele.

I should also point out that I know I'm not faultless in these breakups either, based on my stepdad's old favorite saying: it takes two to tango. I've certainly treated clients worse than I should have at different times throughout my life, and it has cost me relationships. I have to learn from those experiences, and I don't wish Svetlana any kind of ill will.

It's been years since I've worked in the salon full-time, and I miss my regular clients so much. The vast majority of them were the most lovely, loyal, understanding, incredible people I've known. I think about the dozens and dozens of people whose hair I did for years on end and still keep in touch with today. I miss their stories, the honor I felt that they trusted me enough to tell me all about their friends and families, and being able to create new looks for them that would make them feel like their most authentic self.

My clients and I were there for each other through weddings, divorces, deaths, career endings, career beginnings, elections, wins, losses . . . everything. Learning about so many different facets of the business world and humanity itself through the art of hairdressing made me who I am. It's one of the most rewarding multifaceted careers anyone could be so lucky to embark on.

Okay, I know not everyone has these deep and intense feelings about doing hair, so I'll stop being so emo and give you what you were likely hoping to find here: a bunch of great advice about how to get the best hair of your life without making life terrible for the person behind the chair.

1. If you want to develop a long-lasting and healthy relationship with a new hairdresser, don't start off your appointment by listing all the different ways every hair person you have ever been to has fucked up your hair. I always hated it when someone did that, and I suspect many other hairdressers feel the same. It sets an immediate precedent that you might be a difficult client, so try to kick off your new relationship on a positive note.

2. It helps us a lot if you bring in pictures of hair colors you love for us to work off of. Color can be very subjective, and your description alone isn't a safe bet. A visual helps immeasurably, because what sounds like a warm honey blond to you might sound more like a pale ash to your colorist. Photographs ensure a common understanding. The same goes for hairstyles: show an image of what you like, but understand that what you end up with probably won't be an exact replica. Professional photos have the best lighting, hair, makeup, and styling teams behind them, not to mention hours of Photoshop. Plus, everyone's hair grows differently, so it's not realistic to think you'll end up with an exact match. (Not to mention that the whole "Make me look just like her" thing feels a little *Single White Female*. Be inspired by someone else's cut, but make it your own!)

3. I am one thousand percent here for a sexy goth look, but don't ever color your hair black if you think you'll want to go back to your natural color any time soon, or even just want to add some highlights. Whether the black was done by a professional or came from a box (and FYI, box hair color is often the same kind of dye used on clothes), it will take hours upon hours of lightening before it will look anything close to good. I've seen so many ugly, glaring red-orange highlights that take multiple lightening sessions before the hair gets close to any sort of shade you won't hate. If you've gone full black and want to make a change, my best advice is to search out an amazing corrective colorist with a stellar reputation who has about ten free hours to spend only on you. Or cut it all off! I love a good buzz cut.

4. I mentioned this one earlier, but it bears repeating: if you book an appointment with a new hairstylist to fix a hair-color disaster, give that person more than one chance to get it right, especially if you're not giving them a lot of your time. Whenever I inherited a corrective color client, or any job that involved any kind of big transformation, it could take me two or three sessions to get the overall look absolutely slayed. If you feel like it's not quite there but it's getting close, give the stylist another chance. Unless of course after your first appointment there's a total dumpster fire on

your head and the whole time you felt like you were in an episode of *American Horror Story: Salon*. Then you might want to start your search over again.

5. Try not to book Saturday appointments if you can help it. If you can take a little time off from work during the week, that's the best time to go to a salon. Everyone wants a Saturday slot, and a salon will do their best to accommodate as many people as possible, but on weekends even the most well-oiled machine can turn into a scene from *Mean Girls*, except instead of girls tackling each other over a boy in the cafeteria it's stylists and colorists cussing each other out over whose client needs their color rinsed first when the washing stations are mobbed. If your stylist always seems booked within an inch of their life on Saturdays, do everyone a favor and switch up your routine.

6. I love looking at hair-color swatches, and so do most clients, but remember that they can be misleading because the finished colors are applied on fake white plastic hair. If you take a red marker to a piece of white paper it looks much brighter than if you'd used yellow, brown, or black paper. Since most people's hair isn't actually white (and if it is, don't you dare touch that killer Helen Mirren look), those swatches can be extremely inaccurate, not to mention that

a small sample won't give you a good idea of how a color will look all over your head. Swatches are fun for colorists to figure out what your hair color is starting out at, and how we should mix a color to *achieve* what your hair-color vision is, but they won't give you a real sense, and it's better to work off pictures if you have a specific shade in mind. Let us do the color math.

7. My last bit of advice might sound simple, but I think it's the most important. Try to go to your salon appointment calm, clear, and connected with yourself as much as possible. Your stylist is trying to do the same, and if you can start off on this ground together, the experience will be so much better for both of you. Remember, you're not just there for a haircut. You've taken time out of your schedule for self-care—a chance to sit for a bit and let someone help you achieve the confidence that comes with being seen the way you want the world to see you.

Thank you for coming to my written TED Talk on mutually beneficial salon relationships.

CHAPTER 7

TERF WARS

Or, why are trans-exclusionary radical feminists
Dolores Umbridge incarnate?

I can recall three separate occasions standing in line all night with my cousins at Walmart, anxiously waiting for our chance to purchase the highly anticipated release of the latest Harry Potter book. Every single Hogwarts fanatic in our city of forty thousand and the surrounding areas would descend on the store on the eve of the publication date, each of us praying to Dumbledore that we'd be one of the lucky kids whose lottery numbers got chosen, meaning we'd be the first to get to grab the latest adventures of Harry, Hermione, and Ron before the store's inventory sold out.

This wasn't an 80 percent off Black Friday sale—everyone there felt connected in their love for the books. People would dress up in robes featuring the colors of whatever Hogwarts house they identified with (I always knew the Sorting Hat would put me in Gryffindor because—duh) and cheer on those chosen ones who got to rush home and stay up all night, racing to the end of the book to find out the fate of our favorite wizards. Queer and straight, young and old, Black, Brown, and white came together for a night unlike any other, all of us misfits living our best lives beyond the judgmental stares of a very religious community that often didn't understand us.

I'm sure it wasn't quite as emotional an experience for everyone, but for those of us who read the Harry Potter books with pure joy and discovered a secret path to help us find our own internal magic, the feeling of togetherness was palpable. We looked to Harry and his friends for courage to find a way out of all of our own various predicaments. These happy memories run deep for me.

That's why it was so painful when the books' famous author, J. K. Rowling, revealed her views on trans people. Rowling's revelation came as a shock because for much of her career she'd identified as an ally to lesbians, gays, and bisexuals.

I am incredibly proud to be queer and nonbinary, and I'm especially proud and grateful to be part of the larger trans and nonbinary community. This is where I've met some of my greatest teachers and closest friends, like the brilliant Alok Vaid-Menon, who allowed me to unlearn so much of the toxic misogyny I had internalized my entire life. I'm in awe of the strength and resilience of Ashlee Marie Preston, a fearless leader and beacon of hope to so many people in the LGBTQIA+ community, especially in the way she's able to protect younger trans folks and help more people find their path. I wouldn't be who I am without the wisdom I've gained from them, including recognizing and fighting my own internalized transphobia and homophobia that I hadn't even realized were there. I've experienced so much growth and expanded my own capacity for joy through embracing my trans and nonbinary friends, and I want everyone else to have the same opportunities.

Rowling balks at the term "transphobic" being assigned to her, but this comment that she left on a retweet of an op-ed titled "Creating a More Equal Post-COVID-19 World for People Who Menstruate"[1] created a lot of controversy:

"People who menstruate." I'm sure there used to be a word for those people. Someone help me out. Wumben? Wimpund? Woomud?[2]

After many people swiftly pointed out how hurtful her comment was, she doubled down by tweeting:

If sex isn't real, there's no same sex attraction. If sex isn't real, the lived reality of women globally is erased.

I know and love trans people, but erasing the concept of sex removes the ability of many to meaningfully discuss their lives. It isn't hate to speak the truth.[3]

She might not see herself as transphobic, but to many, Rowling officially outed herself as a trans-exclusionary radical feminist, or what's commonly referred to as a TERF. Not only does she refuse to admit how her comments might be hurtful, she also justifies her nonacceptance of trans people as a way to protect the identity of all "biological women" everywhere.[4] TERFs often seek to sow seeds of mistrust and doubt by claiming that if trans women are given the same protections that cis women have, then women's rights will be erased. But in gendering menstruation and birthing as female, she's also erasing trans men and nonbinary people assigned female at birth.

TERFs also often regard trans men as misguided women, completely dismissing their lived realities. Let me be clear: trans women are women, trans men are men, and nonbinary people are as valid and deserving of respect as anyone else. TERF thinking is not just alienating; this zero-sum philosophy is also dangerous—there is more than enough room at the table for everyone, especially people who have already fought so hard to live their truth.

Rowling's Polyjuice Potion recipe must have gone seriously wrong, because not long after those first few social media comments, she suddenly transformed into her own Dolores Jane Umbridge on her accounts, blasting vile rhetoric to millions globally, and then painting herself as a victim when she was presented with the truth.

In fairness, and as someone with my own share of people online telling me to die of AIDS, etc., etc., I'm sure some of the backlash went too far. But whenever I've received backlash, especially if I've hurt or offended the LGBTQIA+ community in some way (like when I made a Bernie Sanders hair gel joke that will forever haunt me online), I'm able to see that I have let people down who looked up to me and that their harsh words are coming from a place of hurt and neglect. I think that for trans and nonbinary fans of J. K. Rowling who felt triggered by her transphobia, the pain was compounded because so many of us turned to her storytelling to escape the suffering inflicted on us. Obviously this doesn't make online abuse okay, but understanding the disappointment that the backlash is coming from is important.

J. K. Rowling has been open about her own past traumas of domestic abuse and sexual assault, and I acknowledge that is really difficult to do. But instead of ending the cycle of harm, I believe she is projecting her hurt and trauma onto other people. As a trauma survivor myself, I know I've done this. But one thing about trauma is that if you don't deal with it, and you continue to project it onto others, it distorts your reality, which is why Rowling only doubled down on her stance after the response to her comments. She even published a lengthy essay on her website filled with her concern about children and teenagers who transition, saying: "I've wondered whether, if I'd been born 30 years later, I too might have tried to transition. The allure of escaping womanhood would have been huge." And: "If I'd found community and sympathy online that I couldn't find in my immediate environment, I believe I could have been persuaded to turn myself into the son my father had openly said he'd have preferred."[5]

Ugh, I wish she'd *accio* her ability to understand trans people faster than Harry *accio*'d his broom during the Triwizard Tournament so he could defeat the Hungarian Horntail dragon.

Because guess what, J. K. Trans people were transitioning when you were a teenager. Likely in fewer numbers, because there were far less developed support systems in place (and those are still severely lacking), but people did it *because they were actually trans* and needed to live as their authentic selves.

If J. K. had been trans, she likely *would* have been able to find community outside of her immediate environment as a teenager, even back then, thanks to the resources her white privilege afforded her long before she became famous. I know how much she loves her rags-to-riches story, but surely with that Exeter University education she was able to hone her research skills. Such seemingly willful ignorance costs trans people their safety, livelihoods, and actual lives.

I wish that was all. Her essay also dives into that tired argument that men will put on dresses and lurk in women's restrooms to assault them if we allow trans people to use the bathroom. I've never heard anything more ludicrous. Trans people are often the ones on the receiving end of horrific bathroom crimes! When you have trans women being forced to use men's restrooms, it makes them vulnerable to harassment. Our culture has normalized violence against trans people to such a point that even peeing and pooping aren't safe. Our society privileges hypothetical nonexistent scenarios over the everyday realities of trans people. We live in a world that prioritizes non-trans people's anxieties over trans people's lives.

Let me be clear again: Trans people aren't what make public spaces dangerous for women. It's the toxic masculinity that parades as protecting tradition and succeeds in maintaining the patriarchy. One easy way to start dismantling the not-even-based-in-reality bathroom argument is to simply get rid of the outdated model of gendered bathrooms to begin with. All anyone needs in order to do their business safely and with dignity is a small, completely enclosed space with a toilet and a door that locks. Who was the sadist who invented those stalls with giant gaps everywhere so that anyone who wants to can peek underneath? Office buildings and other public spaces need to create inclusive bathrooms for everyone by providing layouts that offer both privacy and community safety for all. I'm sure Elizabeth Warren would've had a plan for that, and probably still does.

TERFs would claim there's no need to rethink public bathrooms, because gender dysphoria is new, something society has wrought. But trans and nonbinary people are not new to humanity. What *is* relatively new (in a history-of-the-human-race kind of way) is the concept of the binary gender system as much of the world sees it now. And unfortunately, honey, we have colonialism to thank for that. Ever since England began its colonization efforts in the late sixteenth century, the idea of promoting and advancing the British Crown was synonymous with spreading "civilization" to Indigenous people all over the world—"civilization" meaning white people's customs. British gender norms were regarded as the pinnacle of human evolution, and anything else was "lesser than."

One of the practices of colonialism that people don't talk enough about is eugenics. "Eugenics" comes from a Greek word that translates as "good in birth," and it involves two approaches: preventing "undesirable" or "unfit" groups from reproducing (negative eugenics, like sterilization) and promoting the reproduction of "desirable" groups (positive eugenics). Eugenics is most often associated with Nazi atrocities and genocidal practices during the Holocaust. But many people don't know that eugenics began long before this and was actually rampant in the US.

Here's a brief history for you: Charles Darwin had a cousin named Francis Galton who got super pumped about how Darwin's evolutionary theories played out in humans and really ran with his ideas, but in a bad direction that made the case for a "superior" race of men. In 1883, he published a book called *Inquiries into Human Faculty and Its Development,* and in it he wrote:

> *There exists a sentiment, for the most part quite unreasonable, against the gradual extinction of an inferior race. It rests on some confusion between the race and the individual, as if the destruction of a race was equivalent to the destruction of a large number of men. It is nothing of the kind where the process of extinction works silently and slowly through the earlier marriage of members of the superior race, through their greater vitality under equal stress, through their better chances of getting a*

livelihood, or through their prepotency in mixed mar-riages.[6]

Let's recap, since all that ye olde English is kind of cumbersome to wade through.

Essentially, what he's saying is that individual lives do not matter if they are inferior to a superior race, and as the author, he automatically casts himself—a white British male—as a member of that superior race. Can't you just see him settling back in his big leather chair and smugly puffing on a pipe after spilling this bullshit onto paper with his feather quill pen? (No offense to feather quill pens—those are chic.)

Galton is casually making a case for genocide, and you can draw a straight line from his philosophy here to Hitler's Final Solution fifty years later. Eugenics wasn't some fringe theory—Galton was massively respected and even knighted by King Edward VII in 1909. Eugenics spread from the UK to the US, which became the global epicenter of eugenics in the early twentieth century.

The concept of eugenics relies on controlling reproduction, and since it also favors the group over the individual, it removes anything beyond a strict binary gender structure. Traditional gender norms are created and policed in order to maximize reproduction of people considered most desirable in society (in the context of the US, this has historically been white, heterosexual, cisgender, able-bodied, Christian people). American eugenicists like Paul Popenoe and his American Institute of Family Relations (AIFR) argued that it was women's biological destiny to be mothers and caretakers and that the reason marriages didn't work out was because couples weren't practicing traditional gender norms.[7] Gross!

In the early twentieth century, LGBTQIA+ people began to be targeted by eugenicists, who tried to "fix" us via conversion therapy, lobotomies, and chemical castrations so that we wouldn't tarnish the race. Intersex people and gender nonconforming people were dismissed as evolutionary throwbacks who had to be eliminated from the population in order for the race to thrive. Who gave Galton and his dudebros the license to speak for nature all of a sudden? The world had been evolving on its own—biologically speaking—relatively fine before this asshole. In fact, ever since people started recording history, almost every continent has had some form of culture that allowed room for more than two genders.

In college, gender studies courses first introduced me to people and cultures that express gender differently from the Western binary model. For instance, the hijras in South Asia. They're considered a completely separate gender and community made up of what a Westerner might call trans and intersex individuals and eunuchs, but the community is open to anyone who feels they don't fit on one of the binary tentpoles of male and female. Hijras have a rich and deep history in South Asian culture and mythology, so naturally the Brits hated them and targeted them under the Criminal Tribes Act of 1871, making their existence illegal. What's especially fucked up about this is that the whole reason the British even came to know about the hijras was because one was murdered. An investigation was opened, and when the Brits found out what hijras are, they were so horrified by their very existence that the murder victim became the enemy.[8]

South Asia isn't the only region with genders outside the Western binary. Hawaii and Tahiti call theirs māhū, and Tonga has fakaleiti. And of course there is a long history of Native American two-spirit people in what we now call the US. Humankind is full of rich histories of acceptance as well as disgust and violence whenever white men came sniffing around.

I know we've just blown through history like Sandra Bullock in *Speed*, but please don't be that scared lady who tries to escape early and gets blown up. Just sit tight a second, because I'm sure that by now you're probably wondering what all of this has to do with TERFs.

Well, trans-exclusionary radical feminism gains its roots and warped logic from the same white supremacy ideals that birthed eugenics, because eugenics also considered women inferior to men and maintained that the primary role of a woman in society was to birth children. In fact, defining womanhood solely by the ability to give birth is something done only by sexist eugenicist men! They would argue that women shouldn't go to school or have the right to vote because biologically it would spoil their bodies, which were meant for reproduction.

It's really not complicated. Women deserve equal rights in all areas of their lives—work, healthcare, finance, in every way that men already have those rights. And since trans women are women, the same rights and protections are universally necessary for trans people too.

Apparently TERFs are big sports fanatics because they also have very strong opinions about how trans athletes will change the fairness of sports. But any claim that it's unfair for a trans athlete to play on a team that matches their gender identity isn't based in science and is without merit. The argument against trans athletes ranges from state-level politics all the way to the International Olympic Committee. The debate usually focuses on the false idea that if a person was born with male sex organs, they could have an unfair advantage due to physiological differences like elevated testosterone levels compared to their rivals. But all women have varying levels of testosterone and estrogen in their bodies to begin with; genders don't have an exact quota that hormones fall within. Like any player, trans athletes have varying degrees of ability anyway, and since hormone levels are different, there is no indication that trans athletes will have an advantage.

Not all trans women choose to take hormones, but for the sake of argument, let's create an example athlete here who does. What that means is that she's actually actively suppressing testosterone in her body, so she isn't experiencing the hormone's athletic benefits. What *is* likely reaping benefits, though, is her self-esteem, body image, and overall mental health.

The argument also ignores the fact that everyone has a different chemical makeup of hormone levels that fluctuate throughout their lives, sometimes even monthly. According to the TERFs' own argument, cisgender women with naturally occurring, elevated testosterone levels should be excluded from sports. Which, by the way, is already happening in some sports organizations, and predominantly to Black and Brown athletes from the Global South with high levels of naturally occurring testosterone, like Caster Semenya.[9]

And yet . . . when Michael Phelps began his swimming career, did he have an unfair advantage because he was shaped like a muscular hairless human torpedo, with size-fourteen feet and double-jointed ankles that allow him to move at the speed of Aquaman? Do seven-foot-tall basketball players get banned from playing because of an unfair genetic advantage? No! We just see these as biological attributes that make them more desirable. That double standard makes me angrier than the iconic Scottish mother from the viral YouTube video in which she busts in on her two daughters and proclaims, "Why do some of you not know how to flush the toilet after you've had a shit? *Disgusting!*"

Excluding trans people from athletics is the same type of bigotry that didn't allow women to play professional baseball until 1943 and excluded Black people from professional golf until 1961. And it's the same discrimination as when the International Olympic Committee began to conduct invasive gynecological exams on female athletes in 1968 before switching to laboratory genetic tests to confirm their own rigid definition of gender, a process that continued through 1998. Their rationale behind these so-called gender verifications was to prevent "women with 'unfair, male-like' physical advantage from competing in female-only events."[10] And according to Dr. Anne Fausto-Sterling's book *Sexing the Body: Gender Politics and the Construction of Sexuality*, prior to 1968 the IOC "had long policed the sex of Olympic competitors in an effort to mollify those who feared that women's participation in sports threatened to turn them into manly creatures."[11] Using the guise of biology to justify gender norms that women have to be frail and weak is not new. There is no evidence of sporting advantages in transgender individuals, and sports are fairer with trans people than without.

People aren't dying or being beaten to death when they are included, valued, nurtured, and treated as equals, but what we are seeing is trans and gender-nonconforming kids' bodies policed with an onslaught of right-wing legislation mired in the same white supremacist school of thought that seeks to extinguish anyone who falls outside the narrow interpretation of the gender binary system.

J. K. Rowling likes to cite studies she's read and people she's met who have transitioned back to their birth sex. Yes, this happens, but it is hardly a universal or even common experience. While more than 40 percent of marriages end in divorce, are we banning marriage? She talks about the harm that can be done to a trans child's body by giving them hormone blockers to halt puberty. You know what's way more harmful? Allowing puberty that goes against a child's gender identity to progress and denying that child their self-expression. It's far more difficult to reverse that process as an adult than it is to temporarily halt oncoming puberty if a youth is questioning their gender identity. It gives them time to find themselves as they mature. Hormone blockers are safe. The Mayo Clinic even details their benefits, and the American Academy of Pediatrics has been actively fighting bills being introduced by legislators in multiple states that would not allow gender-affirming medical care for children.

Hormone blockers should be a basic universal healthcare benefit for anyone questioning their gender identity, yet the meds are constantly politicized all over the world. In fact, hormone blockers are routinely given to cis children who have "precocious puberty" (early onset) to delay their puberty. It only becomes a problem when it's about trans kids and legislators hide behind medical-speak as a shield to disguise their prejudice. According to a report in *The Journal of Clinical Endocrinology & Metabolism*, the 2020 Republican primary ballots in Texas included this horrific misinformation: "'Texas should ban chemical castration, puberty blockers, cross-sex hormones and genital mutilation surgery on all minor children for transition purposes, given that Texas children as young as three (3) are being transitioned from their biological sex to the opposite sex.' Even though 'chemical castration' and 'genital mutilation' are not part of gender-affirming care for minors, such wording serves to alarm the general public, and 94.57% of the electors supported the measure. This type of misinformation has led to an increase in threats to clinics and providers of TGD minors."[12]

There's lots of fearmongering, with people also claiming a kid can have gender reassignment surgery without parental consent, which is a complete fabrication.

What you don't hear about as much are the thousands of trans people whose lives were saved by hormone blockers. That's because many journalists like to dig up stories about people who say they weren't old enough to have informed consent when prescribed hormone blockers.

Let me introduce you to a little phrase called "confirmation bias." This is what happens when people have a predetermined idea and seek only a limited amount of data to "prove" their claims. In this case, the goal for these journalists and their supporters is to deny that trans people exist, or to claim that it's possible to stop being trans, so they seek out stories to confirm that. Hate to break it to you haters, but trans people have always been here, and always will be.

Social media discourse also contributes to a continued conflation of youths taking hormone blockers and trans adults taking hormones to transition, but the reality is that folks aren't given hormones to begin transitioning until they are at the age of consent, and they're monitored by doctors and mental health experts. (That is, if they are even lucky enough to have those services available to them—most trans youths don't, and that's a whole other terrible nightmare.)

The only person who can say with any certainty what their gender is, is that individual. We need a healthcare system that validates this, politicians who support trans lives, and people with powerful platforms like J. K. to develop a better understanding of what it means to be a real feminist—one who is able to look beyond their own experiences and privileges and see where others' voices and views are being suppressed. It means lifting everyone up, not continuing to relegate and dehumanize others to allow you a false equivalency in power.

So many fret that the rights of "real" women are going to be erased in the fight for trans acceptance, but Rowling is lashing out at the wrong target. Her argument shouldn't be against trans people, it should be directed at a system that still oppresses all of us: the stale, rigid gender binary.

As hurt and disappointed and angry as I am about Rowling, her views are hardly unique. Being a nonbinary person in the public eye is difficult enough, but having such an important person spreading so much misunderstanding only makes it harder for us to exist safely. I have to worry if I can wear heels in public, in the event someone chases me or I need to make a run for an exit. On the street, I have to monitor where all people are around me at any given moment in case a transphobic stranger tries to assault me. I always need to be paying attention.

I'm in a constant battle with myself to keep from going numb to all the transphobia that exists in my world, from press interviews with clueless journalists to nasty looks I get just trying to buy a cup of coffee. It's a defense mechanism that's easy to slip into, because if I focused on all the horrific things people say about my femininity or gender expression, I wouldn't be able to function. But then I remember everything my friends like Alok and Ashlee do to help people, and know that I have to keep fighting. I have a huge support network, but I want to protect those who don't. And there are a lot.

According to the 2020 *Trans Legal Mapping Report*, which

details a study conducted by the International Lesbian, Gay, Bisexual, Trans, and Intersex Association (also known as ILGA World), forty-seven United Nations member states do not legally allow you to change your gender, and thirty-seven countries have specific criminalization laws against trans people. But even those numbers are slightly misleading. As the journalist Jamie Wareham pointed out in an article for *Forbes*, "It means by extension, transgender people are facing the same penalties [as lesbians, gays, and bisexuals], as their gender identities are being conflated with violations of anti-gay laws. Indeed, in Iran, Saudi Arabia, Yemen, Sudan, the death penalty is regularly imposed for same-sex sexual acts."[13]

In the United States, more anti-trans legislation was debated and passed in 2021 than at any other point in US history.[14] The previous year, 2020, was officially the deadliest year on record for the trans community (especially murders of Black trans women). As of this writing, 2021 is set to break that record.[15] There is a culture of violence where trans people are both blamed for their own deaths and framed as dangerous, even though we are the ones in danger.

Protection laws vary by state, but the Movement Advancement Project found that only 45 percent of our LGBTQIA+ population live in states with a high number of protective policies.[16] The ones that do exist look similar to the Equality Act, which would amend the Civil Rights Act of 1964 to include nondiscrimination laws based on sexual orientation and gender identity. (At the time of this writing, it still hasn't been passed by the Senate.) The Equality Act would protect LGBTQIA+ people from being fired from their jobs or denied housing, education, federally funded programs, or jury service. There are so many rights that most Americans take for granted that trans and nonbinary folks can be penalized for and discriminated against for trying to exercise.

Masculine and feminine energy can be felt in as many varied ways as there are people in the world. We don't inhabit a gender binary but a spectrum. I have felt enduringly receptive, nurturing, unconditionally loving feelings for lovers, friends, and other folks—all feelings that are traditionally associated with feminine energy. I have never felt completely female or completely male, but somewhere in my own space I have found the gender expression that feels authentic to me, and I'm hardly the only one who has journeyed down this road. Everyone should be free to do that for themselves, and to receive healthcare, to get any job they want, and to pursue all their life goals. Cisgender people have no idea what it's like to navigate a cisgender world as a trans person and therefore should not be allowed to make laws and policies for trans and nonbinary people. It's the exact same reason why cisgender men shouldn't be allowed to tell cisgender women what they can and can't do with their bodies.

To put this another way: How can we possibly believe that with over seven billion people on the planet, we'd all fit neatly into only one of two categories? How much damage has been done to humanity by clinging to the binary itself? How many women, femmes, nonbinary, and intersex folks were systematically prevented from an education, from holding elected office, from owning their own property, from living an independent life? It boggles the mind to think of how much bigotry has cost the world by not allowing so many brilliant minds to flourish. We might have had a cure for cancer or have climate change under control by now.

Attempts to silence gender-nonconforming and trans people are nothing less than the attempted erasure of entire cultures, expressions, and humanity, everything that believers in eugenics tried to do. Daily, I hear or read comments like "Nonbinary is completely new and made up" or "Being nonbinary is nothing but a man in a dress" or "God made two sexes. You're just confused." Or way worse—those examples border on politeness compared to the violence and extremism others experience. But we have a human right to feel safe, and, as we say here in the US, the unalienable rights of life, liberty, and the pursuit of happiness, no matter what the bigoted TERFs and radical right-wingers of the world try to do in order to silence us or beat us down.

I'm heartbroken to not be a J. K. Rowling fan anymore. I'm glad her books helped me find a light to crawl towards in some of my darkest childhood times by helping me believe in magic, but I'm even more glad knowing my dollars aren't supporting her anymore. I never will again unless she fully recants her stance, apologizes, and becomes a generous donor to trans activism causes. Until then, later, Dolores.

CHAPTER 8

IMPOSTOR SYNDROME

Or, are we all fakers?

At the ripe old age of twenty-nine, I made my first trip to New York City. It was also the first time I ever went to the Radio City Christmas Spectacular, and the experience was as beautiful, glitzy, and awe inspiring as I'd always imagined it would be after years spent watching the Rockettes' gorgeous routines in the Macy's Thanksgiving Day Parade on TV with my grandma. It had been a lifelong dream of hers to see the famed holiday show live, but she never made it. My trip to New York happened the first Christmas after she passed, and I thought of her during the whole show, getting teary-eyed every single time the Rockettes swung their synchronistic gams to the heavens.

I remember spending a lot of time looking around the theater itself, with its spectacular art deco lobby, marble walls, and the arched orange ceiling in the auditorium that leads your eyes directly to the stage. It's such a storied and iconic institution, and every legendary entertainer you could possibly think of has performed there, but of course my mind went straight to all the divas who'd been up on that same stage: Aretha, Mariah, Britney, Gaga, Adele, Christina . . . I felt like I was in a trance the whole time, and if you'd told me that four years later I'd sell out the same venue as a stop on my own headlining comedy tour, I would have told you that Anastasia Romanov is my mom and I'm going to be the new empress of Russia.

Booking my first international comedy tour didn't happen overnight, and it also didn't happen the same way these opportunities typically work out for comedians. Especially for my comedian friends and clients whose hair I'd done for years in Los Angeles. I knew people who had spent years going to open mic nights, honing their craft and trying to get a comedy career going. I was always supportive of them, but that path had never been my passion. Mainly because after standing behind a chair for eight to ten hours during the day, being a hilarious and fabulously skilled colorist and hair stylist, I had no creative juices left, nor the patience to show up, for an open mic night on the off chance that I might get to perform.

That said, I'd always loved watching stand-up comedy. My

favorites were Margaret Cho, Janeane Garofalo, Lisa Lampanelli, Wanda Sykes, and all the Queens of Comedy. In 2001, during the height of the anthrax scare when people were getting random letters full of a highly lethal white powder, I just about died when Margaret Cho proclaimed at the top of her set, "My first instinct when I receive an envelope filled with white powder ... is *to snort it*! I just won't do that this time."[1]

I was floored. Irreverent drug jokes! Did I actually know back then what cocaine was or how it made you feel? No! But I knew Margaret Cho was the funniest fucking person I had ever heard in my life, and I quickly grew to appreciate the art form of comedy. Nay, heaux, I revere it: the buildup, the joke, punched up by an even funnier one right after it. It was a skill I respected in others, but it wasn't something I thought could ever be my reality, more of a thought like, *I wish I could do that someday.*

Later, that thought started to take a deeper hold as I came into my own with *Gay of Thrones.* I began to wonder if I actually should try my hand at stand-up. But it still felt more like a dream, and any dream is bound to bring up a storm of emotions and concerns about your self-expectations. I remember being a hair colorist assistant and fantasizing about the day when I'd finally be able to take a client of my own back to my station, to create a color the way the client and I decided to do it, not the way my boss told us it had to be done. Along with those dreams came fears too. Would my clients trust in me? Would they believe I could do it on my own, and trust me to fix their hair in case anything went wrong? Whether it's hairdressing or stand-up, I've always had a voice of doubt that questioned not only my worthiness of the opportunities presented but also my ability to perform my work well and have it received well by others.

While I hadn't spent much (well, any) time at open mic nights as one would expect of an up-and-coming comedian, I had unintentionally been doing impromptu comedy shows for my clients at the salon for years. Which ultimately caused me to stumble into my first comedic roll as myself in *Gay of Thrones*, where all of a sudden I was performing a mix of off-the-cuff improvised jokes and scripted monologues that gave me an interesting and unique preparation for my journey into stand-up comedy.

My first taste of doing actual stand-up happened when I went to a comedian friend's show at a gay bar in Silver Lake. *Gay of Thrones* was starting to get noticed, and this friend randomly asked me to do a short five-minute opener for him. All I needed to do afterwards was press PLAY on his laptop to make his own prerecorded introduction appear on a projection screen and then get my ass off the makeshift stage.

I spent the whole day leading up to that moment practicing my set on my clients at work, and I thought I was ready. Wrong. While I was up there, all of the jokes I'd planned ended up bombing, but I realized I was nailing all of the unplanned ones that started popping into my head. My set ended up being a few jokes connected by stream-of-consciousness stories, retelling some of the most fabulous figure-skating tales of all time, but à la me. Like how in 1994 a thirteen-year-old Michelle Kwan gave up an Olympic spot that was rightfully hers so that Nancy Kerrigan could skate, and then Tonya Harding started her long skate three minutes late, claimed a broken lace, and eventually performed to the theme music from *Jurassic* Fucking *Park*.

I went five minutes over, and when I finally finished, I somehow botched the big laptop moment, and my friend had to introduce himself. Looking back, I wasn't that great, but, honey, we all have to start somewhere. The show was brief but long enough for me to fall in love with being on stage and making people laugh. I mean, laughing makes people feel good, and I love making people feel good! Plus, I'm an open book when it comes to the things that have happened to me throughout my life (like, literally, I wrote a very open book about it). Being able to laugh about some of my more embarrassing or absurd moments and then seeing a whole room of people laughing along with me felt pretty healing, even if one or two of my stories could get a little dark.

After that first performance, the pull of the microphone only grew stronger. I still didn't feel quite ready to give comedy a real shot, though, so similar to the marvelous Mrs. Maisel, who in season 1 workshops her jokes in the comfort of parties, I began to practice telling funny stories while doing people's hair. I had the itch, but I was too afraid to say out loud that I wanted to try stand-up comedy as an actual career choice.

I was already doing comedy with *Gay of Thrones*, but that was filmed on camera, not live. If I flubbed my lines, we'd just do another take. Or four. But after a few more seasons of *GoT* and using my clients as a test audience for jokes, my confidence swelled, and I felt ready to try out my own live set, not just a brief opener. Then I booked *Queer Eye* and everything got put on hold.

While we were filming those first two seasons of *Queer Eye* concurrently in Atlanta, it started to dawn on me that I could be funny on cue without a script, and that I had natural comedic timing. My comedy confidence started to feel more palpable than it had before.

After we finished filming, I returned to Los Angeles. Bobby and Karamo were both living there as well, so they and some of the lovely team members behind *Queer Eye* came to support me when I booked my first ever set at a cute bar in Glendale. It was finally time to give stand-up a real shot.

I was scheduled to go on right after *Saturday Night Live* alum Sasheer Zamata, who of course brought the house down because she's a genius. I was petrified as I walked up to the mic. Was I going to get booed off the stage? I had been practicing my set for weeks, and I'd based it around hair school and how all the trials I had to go through were similar to the bureaucracy of competition that Jaslene González overcame to be crowned winner of *America's Next Top Model* cycle 8. Only in my case, the prize was a cosmetology license instead of representation by Elite Model Management, a cover and six-page spread in *Seventeen* magazine, and a hundred-thousand-dollar contract with CoverGirl cosmetics.

I panicked the moment the lights hit my face, and the entire set that I'd memorized vanished from my mind, except the beginning of the first sentence. Which was "Hair school . . ."

I went into a fugue state and launched into a dramatic retelling of the 2018 rivalry between Evgenia Medvedeva and Alina Zagitova. I don't remember the specifics of what I said, but I felt like I was *on*. By the time I finished I still wasn't sure if people liked me or not, but Bobby and Karamo were lol'ing when I ran off the stage into their arms. After that night I was determined to perfect my craft, because I hadn't felt a surge of passion that intense since learning how to tumble during my prolific high school cheerleading career.

I felt like I needed to write a set and perform it as planned, like a *real* comedian. But could I? The same sense of doubt I had when I was learning how to do backflips on a wooden gym floor began to sink in. When I practiced my jokes at the salon, I often found myself abandoning them because someone's highlights were betraying me, and I needed to focus on their hair instead so it wouldn't become a highlighting horror show on Yelp. The less I practiced, the more my fear of failure became real. But also, much like when I learned to tumble, I just forced myself to barrel headfirst into the unknown.

I kept at it, and then the sudden success of *Queer Eye* and my newfound name recognition helped me get my foot the rest of the way in the door. Even though I didn't feel quite ready, I got a comedy agent, and we started reaching out to venues and booking spots for me across the country. Small stages at first, but then they started to grow larger. I had by no means perfected my craft. I was honing it while on the actual job, developing a solid set while booking at the likes of The Improv and Carolines in New York, places so many comedians dream of getting into.

The first packaged show I created was called *JVN and Friends*, and I landed a sponsorship with Hotels.com. The lineup consisted of me as the MC, and I'd open with my own ten-minute set, and then four other comedians would do around ten minutes each, and then I'd come back for another ten- or fifteen-minute bit to create a roughly one-hour-long show. I toured with geniuses like Jaboukie Young-White, Michelle Buteau, Julio Torres, Ayo Edebiri, Naomi Ekperigin, Beth Stelling, and Solomon Georgio. Not only was I learning so many performance tips and tricks on the fly from these incredible comedians, but also we were making sure there were that many fewer straight white men hogging the spotlight. (Seriously, the comedy world is packed with straight white guys. I couldn't even tell you how many, but Dane Cook. Enough said.)

I started to rewrite and deliver my sets—as I'd originally written them, finally—with more flare and comedic sass than I'd ever given before. Each new show inspired me to keep writing and incorporate new jokes, and my unique brand of comedy was beginning to take shape.

One night I had one Stella too many just before going on stage and decided that was the perfect time for my yearly test to make sure I could still do a standing back handspring. In front of a packed auditorium, I executed the move flawlessly, and the applause and cheers made me realize that I had a captive audience not just for my comedy—I could also incorporate a gymnastics routine! I mean, what were they gonna do, leave? Here was an opportunity to combine my hurt inner child, and their need for a father to watch their routines, with my fully formed adult self, who just wanted to train in gymnastics and learn a proper floor routine for the Olympics-obsessed cheerleader within me who refused to die.

I began training the next day. It was the first time I'd worked on gymnastics moves for real since my freshman year at the University of Arizona. I chose the same music that Aly Raisman had used for her 2016 Summer Olympics floor routine in

Rio, a rousing Slavic number called "The Red Poppy: Russian Sailor's Dance," and I decided to use an air track in my show. (For all of you non-gymnastics-obsessed people, that's a long inflatable bouncy track for performing flips on the fly, and it keeps you from snapping your wrists on hard surfaces. Picture it like a blow-up runway.)

After everything I learned on my first tour, I successfully trained my comedic voice and developed my original ten-minute set into several versions of a spectacular hour-long show, complete with gymnastics routines. I booked my first international headlining tour through Live Nation and called it "Road to Beijing." Everyone asked me what the title meant, and I was like, "Duh, I'm doing a gymnastics routine and I want to get into the next Olympics!" Which didn't exactly track since at the time the next Olympics in Beijing were for winter sports, which feature figure skating, not gymnastics. Whatever—I thought it was funny!

For that tour, I still had a couple of comedians in the show with me, which helped when it came to costume changes. (I mean, someone's got to give me cover to take off a leotard, redo my hair, and be ready to give you glamour and comedy ten minutes later.) I made sure that whoever was booked with me on any given leg of the tour was BIPOC, female, and/or queer. Since I am coming from a place of privilege, I want to use my platform to help raise as many diverse voices as possible. I consider myself a human springboard and want all of those comedians to use me and leap as high as possible.

It's normal for a show to grow and evolve the more one performs it, and I found my jokes getting more and more political as 45 continued his destructive path through democracy and human rights. But I loved that through comedy I felt like I could show audiences what I mean when I say, *Sometimes life can be so hard that if I didn't make a joke of it I would be in my mom's basement eating donuts for the rest of my life.*

As the tour continued to sell out venues, I began to wonder if I could become a comedy special queen. What else could I add to my show that would make my routine sing? Could I bring a tent on stage for quick costume changes while broadcasting a video of my cat Harry Larry giving a live weather report? The answers were yes and yes, and I traveled on, through three continents and six countries, performing forty-seven shows in thirty-seven cities. Wow me! Go off!

Despite all of this success right there in my face, literally living through it night after night, I still often had trouble viewing myself as an actual comedian. The entry to this world had felt too easy, and I couldn't fight a gnawing sense that I'd somehow fooled everyone, sneaking in through the back door. How was I selling out the same stages as some of the most iconic people in the comedy world? Being paid to travel to countries I'd only dreamed I would ever be able to visit?

This wasn't just an internal voice I'd made up on my own. Back when I'd first started admitting to people that I was interested in stand-up, I was told that my path wouldn't work. Specifically, I was told this by some comedians who had frequented my old salon, people who had established themselves as successful stand-up comedians around the LA scene. Some had even just sold their first series. When they'd hear me talking about my little pre–*Queer Eye* gigs and joke ideas, they'd tell me I couldn't become a comedian while working in a salon, waiting around for friends to invite me up on stage. They said I had to get out in the world and do open mic nights four to seven nights a week if I ever wanted to be a legitimate comedian, whatever that means.

"You're not experienced enough," some would say. "And your ten needs work." ("Ten" meaning my ten-minute set, but you probably already figured that out.) One particular comedian who came through my salon once told me that I should quit doing hair and focus only on comedy because there were much better comedians than me who never made it while spending their entire careers trying. Meaning that the only way I was ever going to make it was if I devoted my entire life to the craft. In some ways they were right.

I get it. In the world of comedy, there's a very well-worn path one is supposed to take, an established way to keep climbing to try and find success, and it's a brutal mountain. Endless nights of ten-minute sets to near-empty rooms, not getting paid, dealing with hecklers, and praying that the right person might happen to be in the audience and book you for that one next gig that will jump-start everything. And then it rarely ever comes. It's no wonder comedians often struggle with depression and addiction. And it's no wonder that I started feeling like I didn't really belong after I'd found success.

My impostor syndrome would sneak up on me most often while researching different cities I was scheduled to perform in. I planned to talk about the venues I'd be at, find out what the comedy scene was like there, and incorporate a little local flair into my set. But then I'd think about how many other comedians had spent their whole lives trying to do the same thing but never got the chance.

At smaller venues, where I was booked alongside more established comedians, I'd sometimes get paranoid that they were giving serious attitude, like, *Who is this fucking unscripted nobody from* Queer Eye? *He doesn't deserve to be here.* Much in the way I look at Oksana Baiul for her gold medal. (Nancy was robbed, and I don't care who knows it.)

It's possible I was just making it all up. I mean, no one ever specifically said anything mean to me, but I still often felt like people in the industry didn't think that I'd earned my success or paid the proper dues. That I wasn't legit. I mean, when people write about me, they don't refer to me as "Jonathan

Van Ness, comedian." (Well, some people do. In Europe and Australia, I got reviewed as a comedian, and that makes me feel really good.)

It's easy to slip into a shame spiral when you start doubting yourself because of what other people say, and sometimes it's even worse if you're not sure it's all in your head. When a person says something rude to your face about your abilities, you can at least either confront or ignore them and then commiserate with friends who will prop you back up and encourage your goals. But when paranoia starts creeping in that *maybe* people are saying things behind your back, that's when impostor syndrome flourishes.

When that one comedian told me I'd never make it unless I quit my job, I internalized all the pessimism and rejection at first. But the longer I sat with it, I started to take my internalization and turn it into an interrogation. I asked myself what had made the person say that to me. Had they really been trying to help by suggesting I give up everything in my life that paid my bills and focus solely on one thing? Maybe they just had been trying to prepare me for some of the experiences they'd gone through or to show me ahead of time that the comedy world doesn't work out for most people. It was a piece of advice that instilled fear in me, but it wasn't a reality I felt I had to hold on to. What good comes from telling anyone they can't do something on their own terms?

The more I thought about it, the more I realized there are so many variables as to why a person might discourage you from pursuing a dream. Maybe they're projecting their own doubts and insecurities onto you. Maybe they're just being a total asshole. Either way it's a shitty move, because it can feed feelings of impostor syndrome that become pretty debilitating.

Technically, impostor syndrome isn't even an actual disorder. (I mean, the word "syndrome" itself basically just means a bunch of symptoms.) It was first recognized in 1978 by a couple of clinical psychologists who, according to a 2018 article by Megan Dalla-Camina for *Psychology Today*, "found that despite having adequate external evidence of accomplishments, people with imposter syndrome remained convinced that they don't deserve the success they have."[2] It's like if gymnast Aliya Mustafina said, "Oh, I only won the gold in *two* back-to-back Olympic uneven bars finals because the judges didn't notice my feet were half a centimeter off when I landed the dismount that was literally named after me."

If you can't experience the joy and fulfillment of your own accomplishments, it can start to feel like none of it matters, so why bother? And there are any number of reasons why impostor syndrome can manifest. Poor self-esteem from growing up in a dysfunctional family can do it. Any combination of traumas can leave folks with a lingering shame that they don't deserve what they have. Queer people, BIPOCs, and women often feel it because we've been taught our whole lives, whether subtly or overtly, that we're already "less than" others, that our lives don't hold the same value. Other mental health issues, like depression and anxiety, certainly contribute. Or is it our misogynistic culture that ushers in depression and anxiety in the first place?

Some of the most famous, powerful, and privileged people out there admit to feeling impostor syndrome. I like to cover all my bases when investigating a subject, and while I was scrolling through one of my favorite academic resources, InStyle .com, I came across a whole slideshow called "25 Stars Who Suffer from Imposter Syndrome," and it's stuffed with depressing quotes from the likes of Kate Winslet, Jodie Foster, Meryl Streep, and Tom Hanks.[3] They all have goddamn Oscars! A literal gold statue, given to them by peers in their hyper-specific industry and a physical manifestation of belief from others that You. Are. The. Best. If those stars sometimes can't feel their own success, what the hell hope do the rest of us have?

Then again, they're cis white actors who got trophies from a voting body that has been plagued by its own issues of misogyny, racism, and privilege, so maybe they should feel a little shitty about the gold.

There was a hot second in my life when I thought maybe my impostor syndrome could be a good thing, like maybe I could harness it as another way to motivate myself to work harder to fulfill my dreams, but no. Anything with the power to make you doubt yourself to the point of feeling unworthy is something we need to let go of.

The voice in your head that doesn't believe a path is yours to take—for whatever reason—does not have to be the voice you identify with. Hold on to that and do what I do, which is ask my brain, *What are you scared might happen if you try?* If you can dream it, if you can keep working towards it, you can potentially make it a reality.

Let the wise words of Mariah Carey become your mantra:

> *Just hold on tight, and don't let go. You can make it, make it happen!*[4]

It's your choice if you want to actually sing along to the original song.

* * *

Just when it felt like I was getting a handle on stand-up as a career, the entire industry got turned upside down. When I finished the last leg of my "Road to Beijing" tour in Sydney, standing in front of a crowd of almost seven thousand people, I had no idea we were on the edge of a global pandemic that would temporarily halt our trajectory. But I know it's not over for good. I spent a lot of time in quarantine writing fresh material and fantasizing about the day when I can get inside a comedy club and try out all my new jokes and stories. It won't matter if it's in front of a crowd of twenty-five or in a theater of thousands—I'll still be filled with butterflies. Will I remember how to perform? Will people laugh? Will they consider me a stand-up comedian?

Nerves and doubt aren't the same as impostor syndrome, though.

I think the key to defeating impostor syndrome is to realize that having a doubting voice in the back of your mind is totally normal. It would be delusional for me to step in front of thousands of people and start rattling off jokes and not feel nervous.

In fact, for me, I always question my abilities to make sure that I stay on my toes. I have to equally respect all opportunities that have come, because if I ever switch to autopilot, that's when the joy of creating art will die. I've always been laser-focused on succeeding in the exciting things that came my way: becoming a cheerleader, becoming a hairstylist, becoming an entertainer. Each of those opportunities has also presented a lot of barriers, and I always used comedy to plow through them, so in many ways I've been accidentally preparing to become a comedian my whole life.

I made a decision that whenever feelings of impostor syndrome start to creep in, I'll compassionately yet sternly get those nasty little thoughts in line and make them work for me instead of against me. I will use that voice of doubt to remind me to never grow complacent with my work or my artistic growth. The trick is to know when to say, "Excuse me, voice of doubt!! I hear you, queen, but we aren't an impostor. We've been preparing and working for this moment for ages, and you're really doing a number on my digestive system, so I'm going to need you to calm down while we slay. You can pop back in here again next time and remind me that we're nervous just to keep me on my toes, but for now, I got this."

CHAPTER 9

SORRY, KAREN

Or, white fragility/supremacy looks really bad on you

I'm comin' in hot with a triple lutz, triple loop combination of "Hi, it's me, another white person unlearning my white privilege!"

BIPOC friends, I know you do not need to listen to another white person's epiphanies about race and justice, but let me reassure you that I will do my best to stay in my lane and share my experiences from a self-aware and hopefully beneficial perspective. White people, if you're squirming with discomfort already, I've been there too, but this conversation is one we need to have.

I always loved hearing stories about my family's history when I was growing up. It seemed they were always able to overcome so much, like my great-grandmother Mabel, who was born in North Carolina in 1902 and was left to care for her four children alone after my great-grandfather suddenly dropped dead of a heart attack in 1940. Mabel studied hard and passed the bar exam, becoming one of the first one hundred female attorneys in North Carolina, allowing her to make enough money to care for the children.

One of her kids, my grandmother Anne, applied for and was awarded a full-ride scholarship to Duke University. It happened in 1950, after the college hosted an essay-writing contest and her entry won a prize, allowing her to get her foot in the door of one of the best colleges in the country.

After Anne started at Duke, she met my grandfather Tom, whose family owned a newspaper. The two got married and had three children, including my mom. I never got to meet their oldest kid, my uncle, because he died in a tragic car accident. He was only five years older than my mom, who was fourteen at the time. She grew up and eventually met my dad, who also came from a family that had seen its share of challenges.

My dad's dad was raised primarily by his mother. Her first husband had been an abusive alcoholic, so she divorced him back in a time when divorce relegated you to instant pariah status. She worked through abject poverty, eventually meeting a partner who would later marry her. His name was Louie. They raised their family together and that gave my grandpa a shot to change the trajectory of his life. Using the work ethic they instilled in him, my grandfather was able to pull himself up by the bootstraps, as we like to say in the Midwest. He became a doctor, and served in a medical unit in the Korean War.

These stories filled me with pride about their strength and resourcefulness, and all of their actions that allowed me to have my own chance at success. I always told anyone who would listen about my grandma who went to Duke; I thought it was the coolest story, one that gave me the belief that I too could do anything I put my mind to.

But as I grew older, it became clear to me that white privilege was a very real engine that helped give my family their boosts in life. My eyes were just starting to open to America's rigged system when, in 2012, I returned to my hometown—which is about 97 percent white—with my first serious boyfriend.

This early love of my life, whom I called Sergei in my first book, is a Black man from Louisiana, and falling in love with him changed the way I saw race in America. Before Sergei, I had never noticed when a retail clerk tailed a person of color to make sure they weren't stealing. I waved off the *Are you serious?* look on Sergei's face when I'd bring pot into the car with us, not realizing that while marijuana was a normal item for me to take on any trip, it could have potentially messed up Sergei's life or even gotten him killed because of the way police target Black drivers.

I know it shouldn't have taken dating a Black person for me to recognize the severity of systemic racism. I feel gross about that, and it's a big part of why I'm writing this. We live in such a race- and class-segregated society that it often takes these personal relationships to wake us up. But hopefully by now we've all heard stories and been made aware of the issues that BIPOC face, and we need to take responsibility to educate ourselves and be proactive about racial equity rather than wait to develop an intimate relationship with a BIPOC to care.

Sergei and I had been dating for a couple years when I brought him home to meet my family. My brother was getting married, and as soon as we arrived, my grandmother took one look at us and said, "Thank God you're gay," with a cute old-lady chuckle. It took a few moments to dawn on me that what she meant was, had Sergei and I been a cishet interracial couple, it would've caused quite the stir. She'd said it in a lighthearted way, but essentially she'd meant that since we're gay I'd already caused "quite the stir." So . . . it all evened out, I guess?

My grandma was from a different era and it often showed through in comments like that. She held racist views passed down to her that I have to believe in her heart of hearts she knew were wrong but went along with anyway. It hurt to hear it then, and it even hurts saying it now. Loving someone who has racist beliefs is an uncomfortable relationship to navigate. It doesn't undermine my love for her, but I wish I had been more able to challenge her on her beliefs and change them.

Later that night at the rehearsal dinner, another family member asked Sergei if he was nervous for the wedding day. Since I was a part of the wedding party, he'd have to fend for himself among the guests, who were all white. To try and lighten the mood, Sergei responded, "Oh, I'll be fine. I'm used to being the only Black person in a room."

Without skipping a beat, the person responded, "That's why we got fried chicken tonight."

I dropped my fork, mortified, but Sergei laughed and grabbed my leg under the table as if to say, *It's fine—don't make a scene.*

It was only out of respect for his silent request that I didn't, but through loving Sergei, I witnessed all of the microaggressions and outright racist comments he dealt with on a daily basis. I came to understand that there were many things I could do with impunity that Sergei would not dare do. I began to recognize my own white privilege in so many different scenarios.

Seeing through the eyes and experiences of the man I loved made me sick. How could I have been so naive? Sergei is someone I will always love, and even though our romantic relationship didn't work out, he's still a large part of why I'm working every day to pull back my own assumptions about history and privilege in the United States. I also know that these are lessons I will continue to learn for the rest of my life.

When I began some of my research into our country's past, I was shocked by how much I hadn't known. All states (even the Northern ones) practiced segregation in restaurants, banks, theaters, clubs, and the like up until the Civil Rights Act of 1964, and it's shameful that I didn't learn this until much later in life. I knew that schools weren't integrated until the '60s, but I thought that was only in the South. I didn't know that Black women didn't get the right to vote until 1965 with the passage of the Voting Rights Act. I'd always thought women—all women—had already won that right. I remember studying the women's suffrage movement in school, and not once did my teacher say, "Btw, white ladies only."

That example is one of the biggest issues facing our reckoning with white supremacy and systemic racism: our country's history is taught in schools in a way that's distorted and full of outright lies. The United States was founded by invading an occupied land and killing and displacing millions of Native Americans, followed by a reliance on the transatlantic slave trade starting in the sixteenth century. These two genocides have consequences that carry on to this day.

I'd like to hope that, with some of the more recent social justice reckonings, schools will be changing the way they teach US history, but in some states it's just getting worse, with Republicans outright banning the study of critical race theory (CRT) in some state public schools and colleges; and many more conservatives are trying to pass similar legislation.

Most people who want to ban CRT don't even know what it actually is. It's simply an area of academics that lays out the facts about the way the US was literally built on the free labor of enslaved people, and how that evil has never been undone. (You can see why it makes Republicans so uncomfortable.) CRT is about all of the nightmare injustices we've been discussing throughout this book, like the effects that chattel slavery and Jim Crow laws have on modern America. How banks would not grant mortgages to Black and Brown people who wanted to buy homes, and how education systems didn't allow for BIPOC students. How mass incarceration is a direct descendant of slavery, originally designed so that police could capture and return enslaved people.

I thought it was awful enough that I was taught at an impressionable age that Native Americans and settlers came together for the first Thanksgiving, and then slavery happened, and it was bad, but then Abe Lincoln came along and ended it, and soon everything was fabulous. Revisionist history is one thing, but the outright banning of specific studies is nothing short of fascism.

American kids aren't educated about what really took place in order for modern America to exist. Or all the ways in which segregation was and continues to be practiced. Or that a blood quantum for Native Americans—a measurement of how much "legitimate" Native American blood is in the descendant of an Indigenous person that's then calculated to limit their citizenship—still exists to this day. Another rule that was used in several states at the turn of the century, called the one-drop rule, said that if you had "one drop" of Black blood you would be treated legally as such. This also had ramifications for people who were Native and Black, as one's Blackness could prevent them from having tribal citizenship.

Dr. Elizabeth Rule, director of the AT&T Center for Indigenous Politics and Policy, which is the only university-based research center in Washington, DC, dedicated to Native American, Alaska Native, and Native Hawaiian issues, explained to me why. "It is used as a population tracker," she said. "A lot of tribes rely upon blood quantum to determine their own citizenship and membership and inclusion in the tribe. But it goes back to efforts to eradicate Native people. The idea [being] that Native people would eventually intermarry and have children with non-Native people to the point that they literally bred themselves out of political existence—ceased to exist as tribal nations with sovereignty and all the rights and privileges thereof. And therefore, the United States would be rid of its federal obligation to fulfill its treaty obligations."[1]

* * *

The more research I did, the more I began to see how all of the things I hadn't known about directly affected the advantages my family had access to that, say, Sergei's grandmother didn't. Duke University didn't allow Black students to enroll until 1963, so his grandmother wouldn't have even been allowed to apply for that scholarship my grandmother won.

While doing this research, I discovered the term "social capital," which isn't about money but rather about access to social relationships that can gain you entry to or assistance from an institution. Suddenly I understood just how much my entire family and I had benefited from exactly this, while the United States was simultaneously creating barriers for Black people's upward economic mobility, and how the ripple effects are still being felt to this day.

In 2015, during Trump's rise to the presidency while rolling out his first campaign, it became clear to me that a close family member—let's call him Yohan—planned to support him. I was aghast and knew it was time to start tackling some difficult conversations. With an HIV+ queer person as a family member, how could Yohan . . .

Oh, fuck it. It was my dad.

How could *my own father* support Trump—a clearly racist, homophobic, and transphobic monster?

Just like in many other families across the country, the election brought my relationship with my parent to a whole new low point. I told him about the genocides perpetrated by the government against Native Americans, Black people, Asian Americans, LGBTQIA+ people. But all of my points were easy for him to brush off as ancient history, with no bearing on the America we now inhabit.

"That was back then," he'd say dismissively, along with the phrase "I don't see color," which is one of the subtly racist things that I hear a lot of white people say. They think it comes from a good place, but it actually dismisses the experience of BIPOC. You're saying you actually cannot or will not see the pain they are living with because of how systems treat them because of the color of their skin.

I'd been extremely close with both my dad and my stepfather but lost the latter to cancer, so I wanted to avoid cutting my relationship off completely with the former. He'd always been active in my life in the way many divorced dads are. While I was growing up, we spoke daily, and I spent every Wednesday night as well as every other weekend with him. Even if things were rocky between us as adults, I already knew the pain of never being able to speak to a parent again, and I wanted to at least try and experience some genuine closeness with him.

That said, nobody in my life has ever been able to piss me off quite like my dad. He openly admits that he would have bullied me mercilessly if we were peers, once telling me, "If we had gone to the same high school at the same time, I would've been your worst nightmare."

But I'm an adult now, and with that comes the understanding every kid has to face someday: that our parents have their own baggage, that they are flawed like every other human and not the perfect people we thought they should be while we were growing up.

So I try to look at the good things in him. I know that I got his clever sense of humor as well as his ability to process information quickly, and I'm grateful for those qualities. As someone who once yanked me out of an evening gown in absolute panic when I was young, he now wears ally T-shirts and pride shirts, and keeps a rainbow collar on his dog. He has made progress in terms of his view on LGBTQIA+ people and the discrimination we face, and since I was able to witness that change in him, I'm convinced there can be more. He is someone I want a strong relationship with, and I deeply want him to understand where I'm coming from so that we can get to that point.

But our fights after Trump got elected eventually brought us to a breaking point. By the way, after I begged for months my dad says he didn't vote for Trump in either election but does emphatically support the conservative platform, which to me is one and the same. And a third-party vote in each of those elections was a waste to vulnerable people. The only resolution we could come to that seemed like it wouldn't permanently destroy our ability to speak to each other was an agreement to not talk about politics.

That lasted literally no time at all. I kept fighting because I could not give up on trying to help him see the modern-day realities of white privilege and the ongoing systemic racism plaguing our country.

As the Trump presidency slugged along with a thick trail of slimy corruption in its wake, the gap between us continued to grow. *Queer Eye* had taken off, and my profile had risen dramatically, which meant photo shoots, impromptu hosting gigs, interviews, press tours, all of it making it harder and harder to get quality time with both him and my mom. (Certainly harder than my life as a hairdresser or drug addict had ever made it before.)

Dad attributed all of the growing distance between us to my schedule and blamed that for getting in the way of us being able to maintain our relationship. In truth, though, the distance was more intentional on my side. I needed to set healthy boundaries for myself. If he can love me, yet still support policies that hurt people like me, how can I just chat with him about cats and work?

This was hardly his only weak spot. My dad had a front-row seat to my own development as I was growing up. Even if I expressed myself in ways that felt foreign to him, how could he not see or do anything about all of the external influences that were so clearly affecting me? As I grew older, my name became synonymous with "faggot" at school, and adults stood by, either unsure of how to help or simply unwilling to intervene. I was neglected by most every group of people available to me, from the church to coaches to my peers, all of it amplified by the AIDS epidemic and the messages I heard about gay men contracting the disease. The isolation made my lived experience grueling. All the systemic cruelties that I was up against should have been clear to my father then. How could he still not see them for others?

My dad's minimization of all of this has always been one of the largest hurdles keeping me from fully connecting with him. These days, anywhere from once to seven times a year, I try to see how far he's come in his thinking, to see if any of the truths I've exposed him to—via conversations or articles I've sent or documentaries I've asked him to watch—have finally sunk in.

They haven't fully. My dad is a bit more curious to have these discussions than he once was. In conversations about race, my dad often brings up the same defensive examples of ways in which he and my grandparents were kind to Black people, including their housekeeper and gardener, as if that would rule out any chance of him being complicit in our country's entrenched systemic racism. When, in fact, it should be more proof about the systems I try to explain to him in the first place.

I wish he'd listen to my *Getting Curious* interview with activist and Black Lives Matter cofounder Alicia Garza, who explained how domestic work has its roots in the legacy of slavery, and that it's a job still not federally recognized. "Under slavery, it wasn't employment," she told me. "It was enslavement.... And unfortunately, a lot of the conditions that originated under enslavement are still in this industry now.... Domestic work and agricultural work ... isn't covered by most federal labor protections. So that means so many domestic workers in this country don't have access to overtime, sick pay, sick days, and ... this has a lot to do with how this industry began.... We're still fighting for the same kinds of basic rights and dignity and respect that is needed."[2]

I explained to him that my grandfather's life had been forever improved by his ability to attend medical school, become a doctor, obtain a mortgage to buy a house, build wealth, and pass it down—all things that were infinitely more difficult for a Black person to achieve, thanks to extremely limited options when it came to higher education and the racist actions of the Federal Housing Administration, which actively practiced redlining to segregate Black families and communities.

I told him how if an independent Black community did manage to grow and thrive, it risked becoming a target for destruction. Seneca Village, in what's now Central Park, was seized by eminent domain and torn down in 1857. White mobs invaded a Black neighborhood and started the Atlanta race riot of 1906. It happened again with the Tulsa Race Massacre of 1921, which resulted in many, many murders and the complete torching of what was then the wealthiest Black neighborhood in the country.

Besides the irreplaceable loss of life, the wealth, homes, and possessions that were destroyed in these events were never restored. The communities were left to rebuild with no help from the government. The violence went on to become the basis of why the FHA decided to discriminate against people of color when it came to home loans. White people destroyed their neighborhoods, and Black people were punished for it. Understanding the context of this history is paramount for all people, but especially white folks, so they can begin to see how many government systems today still operate to the detriment of Black and Brown people.

But for my dad, he can agree with many of these things that I've just explained but ultimately gets up in arms saying he doesn't like the word "racism" and that he is not racist. My attempts to educate him about white privilege just felt like attacks on him and his parents' memory and everything they had worked for, and it's an all-too-common response in families across the country. Understanding your complicity can feel like being identified as a bad person, but this isn't an attack; it's an act of love. I want to live in a country that is built not on repression, lies, and exploitation but on equity and love. How can we even begin to right a wrong that people refuse to acknowledge?

From the inception of slavery in the US South to the Civil War to today, there has been a concerted effort to minimize, dismiss, and simply not educate people on the evils of chattel slavery. No responsibility has ever been taken by the US government to remedy the human toll on Black Americans. That is a responsibility all non-Black Americans and our government must take on.

This isn't about personal guilt and shame. That's what makes so many white people unable to look at white privilege and white supremacy—this idea that if those horrors are acknowledged, it makes them and their ancestors culpable. And that's true. White people (including me) have all been culpable, through the actions of all their ancestors who made these atrocities come to fruition. It doesn't feel good to know that. It creates a sinking pit in my stomach that I want to push away. But I fight that urge. I need to confront this within myself, but it doesn't end there either. This is a systemic issue, and that means entire systems have to change, not just one person. Not me, not you, no individual can be responsible for or correct the horrors of racism in the US. We have to be in this together.

I got a chance to interview the brilliant historian and lawyer Dr. Robert Icenhauer-Ramirez before he passed away, and he told me that founding fathers like Washington and Jefferson and Madison all recognized that slavery was evil, but "they didn't know how to deal with it. They didn't have the ability to abolish slavery at the Constitutional Convention, even though a lot of them would have liked to."[3]

Boo-fucking-hoo for them and the other white people who saw injustice happening but were hesitant to do anything about it. "As you study the Civil War . . . Lincoln tiptoes around the issue of slavery because he doesn't want to alienate the people," Dr. Icenhauer-Ramirez told me, though he was also quick to point out that Lincoln was against slavery and just biding his time until he found the right way to justify its abolition. Still, fighting for the North did not automatically mean you were an abolitionist. Dr. Icenhauer-Ramirez confirmed that that most people fighting for the North were fighting to preserve the Union, not to free enslaved people.[4] If the Union were divided, it would make the country more vulnerable to the United Kingdom and other foes.

Look, I'm the first to acknowledge that our painful past does not need to determine our future, but when it comes to racial injustice, the whole of the United States is responsible and must make amends to BIPOC. Until that happens, this country cannot heal. I know it's uncomfortable for white people to face the evils of what happened here. But that discomfort is nothing compared to the actual experiences of oppression that

BIPOC are facing, and that's why we have to push through. Black women are three times more likely to die during childbirth than white women.[5] One in seven Black adolescents have had a parent incarcerated, and Black people are imprisoned at a rate five times that of whites.[6] This is because of the institutional and cultural disregard for Black lives, which we must end. The US will never be the home of the free while so many of our citizens are treated this way. And even if these atrocities don't affect you directly, it's only a matter of time before you or a loved one becomes targeted in our faulty "justice" system.

I can't let my family, whom I love, keep believing that they bear no responsibility. I want to keep having these conversations with friends, family, and ultimately elected officials until reparations are made and white supremacy and privilege are dismantled. I like to think we'll see it in our lifetimes. White people can't stay silent about acknowledging our own complicity. White supremacy isn't just about white people, but no white person is exempt from it either. This system seeks to hoard power, money, and influence—and if we don't actively subvert power structures in our daily lives, these structures will continue to oppress and harm all marginalized people.

It's like what my friend Ashlee Marie Preston says: "white supremacy will eat its own young."[7] LGBTQIA+ white folks, disabled white folks, and white folks living in poverty are often marginalized and harmed by these same white supremacist structures, from police brutality to employment discrimination and homelessness, but nowhere near as often or as harshly as these same cruelties affect Black people. White supremacy is enduringly evil and doesn't care for anyone or anything as much as it cares about maintaining systems of power, which is why white people and folks who benefit from it have to work harder to stop it.

I think almost anyone can be aware of their privilege whatever it may be—white privilege, male privilege, cis privilege, able or size privilege—and try to spread opportunity more evenly. Even if that means one painful conversation after another over the dinner table each night. It could mean finding more educational resources for yourself and your loved ones, it could be inviting loved ones to come along with you as you advocate for voting rights, it could be donating to mutual-aid organizations that directly support BIPOC going through hardships, and supporting or buying from Black-owned businesses. There are ways big and small that we can become more aware of white privilege and the white supremacist structures that still yield violence and harm towards those who need protection most.

I'm not saying I'm perfect, know it all, or have done enough. This process of unlearning so much of what we thought was true is similar to processing grief—it comes in stages. The idea of "the land of the free" is a lie taught to uphold white supremacy. Understanding US history requires a far more nuanced conversation than many white folks are willing to have, and I'm working on accessing more radical love and acceptance with folks who don't agree with me so I can keep engaging and try to be a part of healing, equity, and solidarity with BIPOC. We are all deserving of the so-called American dream, that promise of life, liberty, and the pursuit of happiness. But those are only myths as long as the racist tools of the government still exist. Education and healthcare systems have to be reinvented so that they honor truth and serve everyone equally, and police brutality, mass incarceration, housing instability, and poverty must end. Only then can the American dream become an American reality.

CHAPTER 10

THE HIV SAFETY NET

*Or, whose dick do I have to suck to get more
support for HIV+ people in our country?*

Contracting HIV most likely saved my life. I was devoted to self-destruction through sex and meth addictions throughout my early twenties, and eventually I would have either overdosed, become more involved with narcotics and gotten arrested, or gone home with the wrong guy and gotten murdered. I know that sounds extreme, but that's meth and chemsex. I was on a downward spiral, and discovering that I was HIV+, while emotionally devastating, was ultimately the final straw. I knew recovery was possible, but I had to find a path that would lead me there.

I was living in Missouri at the time, working as an independent contractor at a salon, with only a few months left before I'd be kicked off my mom's insurance on my twenty-sixth birthday. I was also dealing with the death of my stepfather, a severe depression, and a breakup, and through all of that I had to deal with the emotional fallout and practical logistics of my diagnosis, like how to get continued access to the lifesaving antiretroviral therapy—ART—that would bring my HIV infection to an undetectable status.

The time it takes for an HIV infection to cause fatal or life-changing complications is different for each person who contracts it, but it's universally true that the faster you can achieve and maintain an undetectable viral load through uninterrupted medication intake and doctor support, the more likely it is that you can live a long, healthy life, anywhere from fifty to seventy-five years from the time of infection. And as an undetectable person, you pose zero risk of transmitting the virus sexually, though I didn't know that then. The undetectable = untransmittable movement hadn't been scientifically accepted yet.

HIV medications do not come cheap. In fact, they're prohibitively—no, *criminally*—expensive. The costs remain high because, generally, the most effective HIV drugs with the fewest side effects aren't generic. And when drugs do finally go generic, it takes multiple versions within any one drug category to finally get those prices down. Once my health insurance ended, I knew I was going to need some kind of government financial assistance, but I soon found that getting anything out of Missouri at the time was like trying to get me to be interested in golf—it just wasn't happening.

The nurse who delivered my diagnosis had mentioned something about California having a good HIV safety net, and after a quick Google search I discovered the steps I needed to take in that state to get great medical care: I needed to sign up for the AIDS Drug Assistance Program (ADAP) and apply for Ryan White HIV/AIDS Program funding while waiting for my Medi-Cal to kick in—the state's Medicaid program for folks with limited incomes—all punctuated by a doctor taking me in at a clinic run by the AIDS Healthcare Foundation (AHF), where anyone with limited or no income could receive care.

I wasn't destitute, but I certainly wouldn't say that I was living comfortably either. So I stole/borrowed some money from my grandfather and hightailed it across the country to the West Coast in my Kia Rio.

Once I got to Los Angeles, I rented an apartment, found work in a salon, and began signing up for all of the different available programs that I could. It might have been easier than searching for healthcare access in Missouri, but I still ended up crying in the fetal position in front of my laptop in what felt like at least four hundred different times while trying to enroll in all of them, because navigating confusing government-run websites to access care so that you won't die or accidentally spread a virus that could kill someone else should you ever want to have sex again is just a tad overwhelming, to say the least.

Anyone who's ever had to deal with a .gov website knows that they're absurdly difficult to navigate and seem to purposely try and hide every bit of crucial information one might need. Oftentimes, after I'd finally found and finished filling out the correct form, I'd hit SEND only to be greeted by the forever-spinning pinwheel of death, or the screen would crash for no reason and I'd have to start all over again.

Once I'd finally signed up for the myriad of programs that would pay for most of my medication and doctor visits, everything was easy and stress-free, and nothing bad ever happened to me again. The end. *Just kidding.*

Each year after that, with my birthdate as my deadline, I had to submit all of my tax documents and reapply for the programs. If I didn't complete them on time, I could lose access to my medications and care. It was a miserable experience, but I now understand how easy I had it compared to so many other HIV+ people in the US who need these same programs. I didn't know it at the time, but I was tapping into something called the HIV safety net, a series of legal benefits designed to help people with HIV/AIDS. While they've helped me and millions of others, there are still so many hurdles to accessing them. Luckily, in many states there are social justice warriors, like the ones you'll meet over the course of this essay, who work hard to clear the path so anyone with HIV/AIDS can get the lifesaving medical care that they both require and deserve.

I first heard the phrase "HIV safety net" when I read an op-ed by Dr. Celeste Watkins-Hayes, a sociology professor at the University of Michigan who studies HIV/AIDS, race, poverty, and government funding, among many other things. After reading my story, she recognized all of the steps that I'd written about as they relate to her studies of Black women navigating the same system. After I read her article, I knew I had to have her on *Getting Curious* so we could discuss her research.

Dr. Watkins-Hayes pointed out during our interview that before an uninsured and/or low-income person can even get to a place where they're ready to accept the support of the HIV safety net, there needs to be a fundamental cognitive shift in thinking. For me, it was pretty immediate. I was terrified, and I didn't want to die and knew I needed to get ART medications into my body faster than figure skater Sarah Hughes seized her moment to win the gold at Salt Lake in 2002. A long program only takes four minutes, and that was about all the time I needed. Going into a denial space about my HIV diagnosis was not an option.

For the Black women Dr. Watkins-Hayes focuses much

of her research on, though, many were living in a context of multiple challenges and disadvantages. For these women, as she put it, "HIV might not be the thing that you prioritize to address first. You might be grappling with an addiction. You may be grappling with severe depression, anxiety. You may be homeless. So those might be more pressing concerns such that you don't immediately get on medication. And the other issue is just absorbing the fact that you're living with HIV. And for people who are asymptomatic, their view may be, 'Well, I don't feel sick, I don't look sick. I'm just gonna pretend like it's not there or grapple with my other challenges first.'"[1]

Right off the bat, she identified three other scenarios here that need their own safety nets: addiction, mental health, and experiencing homelessness, all of which are rampant in the US. But as she also pointed out to me later, people in power have had a hard time with the concept of safety nets, going all the way back to people in poverty in the 1600s: "There's a concern with free riding and fraud, and a desire to punish the poor as a way to incentivize work. It's necessary for the engine of capitalism to work."[2]

Yikes, and worth digging into more, but I don't want to get off track because before we can look at the steps within the HIV safety net, we also need to look back at the history of the virus itself and just how difficult it was to get any help at all in the beginning. It was considered a gay disease ever since its discovery in 1981, so politicians didn't want to touch it. It was up to the gay community, many of whom were dying in historic numbers, to try and mobilize support.

Like I brought up back in chapter 3, it took four more years and thousands of deaths before Ronald Reagan even said the word "AIDS" in public. And while Rock Hudson's death caused a lot of Americans to start paying attention to HIV/AIDS, it was a brilliant kid named Ryan White who helped educate the larger public about the disease. He was a thirteen-year-old boy who acquired HIV from a blood transfusion and unwittingly—but very bravely—became the poster child for AIDS awareness when his school refused to allow him to attend after his diagnosis. His family's fight against the administration became national news, and he was finally allowed to return to school. He and his family continued to advocate for AIDS awareness and education, and when he died in 1990, one month shy of his high school graduation, Congress passed the Ryan White Comprehensive AIDS Resources Emergency (CARE) Act, a federally funded resource program for people with HIV and AIDS. Technically, it expired in 2013, but Congress continues to fund it. It's now the largest federally funded AIDS assistance program in the country and an essential part of the HIV safety net.

George H. W. Bush was president at the time and signed the CARE Act into law, which is great, but the cynic in me still believes it was just optics. Much in the same way that his son, George W. Bush, many years later said that he was concerned about HIV/AIDS in Africa. He said he'd been convinced that the US needed to help out after his daughters, Barbara and Jenna, became concerned about so many children being orphaned after the death of their parents, so he signed the President's Emergency Plan for AIDS Relief (PEPFAR), a five-year, $15 billion global initiative that provided prevention, treatment, and care services to several countries, primarily in sub-Saharan Africa.

I'm sure the orphan story is partially true, but as Dr. Watkins-Hayes pointed out, "There was also a national security threat. If an entire generation of adults is wiped out from the epidemic and you're left with countries of orphans and old people, you're left with an unstable region with spillover effects. The concern is that it would be particularly destabilizing in ways that could have effects in the rest of the world."[3]

I'm also highly skeptical that George W.'s concern was sincere given that there were folks being orphaned due to HIV/AIDS right here in the US too, and the government wasn't rushing to put a support system in place. As journalist Linda Villarosa pointed out in a 2017 *New York Times* article titled "America's Hidden H.I.V. Epidemic," "Black America, however, never got a PEPFAR. Though the numbers were much lower than in Africa, the new HIV/AIDS infection rates in parts of our country rivaled those on the continent the program was created to save. Yet while buckets of money went overseas, domestic funding for HIV/AIDS remained flat, and efforts to fight the disease here were reduced to a poorly coordinated patchwork affair."[4]

Today, Ryan White funding is great at plugging the holes left in states where Medicaid or the Affordable Care Act haven't been expanded, and while the program is federally funded, it's up to each individual state to create its own system of HIV/AIDS care. The government doesn't just take the money each year and divide it up equally. That wouldn't make sense, since you don't want a state with a small HIV+ population, like Alaska, to get the same amount of money as states like New York and California, which have much more significant numbers and therefore much more need.

But. It's up to states and localities themselves to ask for the money based on their HIV numbers and then create their own plans for spreading those dollars around. And the state you happen to live in completely shapes how those services are built and made available. If you're in a liberal blue state with a strong LGBTQIA+ community involved in the conversation about how Ryan White funding gets allocated, you have a much better chance of getting access to care. If you're in a red state that's more conservative, the experience is going to be very different. And by different, I mean super fucking difficult.

(Obviously that's not just for the HIV safety net—the same goes for any safety net service designed to support disenfranchised communities.)

I once had an awful healthcare experience while visiting a red state. I wasn't acting out with my addictions at the time, but one day I found myself invited to an orgy with a no-hard-drugs policy (we love some responsible revelry), and I thought, *Why not?* I knew it was a slippery slope with my past of sexual compulsivity, but the invite came from a trusted friend, and *Queer Eye* was going to debut soon, so I thought, *Hunty! This might be your last shot. There's no meth involved—go get your sex positive life on!*

By the time I left the party I felt really happy. I'd had a great group sexual experience that didn't devolve into a meth nightmare. But the next day, my penis was decidedly unhappy. In fact, it felt like it was on fire, and I was convinced I'd gotten instant gonorrhea from my little adventure.

I was used to dropping into my local health clinic and getting the medicine required to clear up any STI that came along, so I found the nearest drop-in to my hotel, told the nurse what had happened, what I suspected, and that some azithromycin would clear it right up. If she'd be kind enough to write me a prescription, I'd be on my way.

The disgust was written all over her face. "We don't do that here," she snapped. "We're going to have to test you. May I also suggest that in the future you don't suck a bunch of different dicks at the same time."

I wanted to remind her that I wasn't there for oral gonorrhea and that the problem was in my dick, but instead I said, "Excuse me, do you want me to come up in here and lie to you about what I've been doing, or would you like me to tell you the truth, which will only serve to better help your community by stopping an STI from spreading?"

I felt myself getting even more worked up.

"The way you are talking to me right now is inexcusable. If I was a straight man and came in and told you, 'I fucked seven different women,' would you be saying the same thing? No, absolutely not. Now, unless you want a much bigger issue here, you are going to fucking treat me like a human being, and then treat my gonorrhea."

My outburst worked and she became more professional, even though I could still see the homophobia in her eyes. "We will have to actually test you first," she said. "I'm not just writing a prescription without proof."

That was fine with me and completely fair, considering she'd never seen me before as a patient. And after all that, the test came back negative anyway. Yay me! It was just some general penis irritation from all the fun I'd had!

Another time, when we were shooting *Queer Eye* in Missouri, I was due for my quarterly blood work, which keeps an eye on my undetectable status, so my usual doctor sent a prescription for my lab work to a local clinic. I wasn't expecting a deeply thorough medical examination, just more of a mini checkup until I could see my regular doctor back home, but I still tried to covertly request an anal pap during our initial discussion, which is a standard part of my normal healthcare in Los Angeles because I'm a busy person with no time for bum cancer.

The nurse looked at me like I was out of my mind, and the doctor said, "We don't do that here. No one does that. I've never heard of anyone doing it."

Thank God I used to be a rural male cheerleader and I can withstand awkward embarrassment like nobody's business, because I didn't have it in me to fight that day. I just got up and walked out of the clinic.

It's shocking to me that in twenty-first-century America there are still doctors with licenses who would try to shame their patients. One of the main tenets of the Hippocratic Oath is "Do no harm or injustice" to your patients. Those two did both that day, and with prejudice rooted in homophobia and both puritanical and uninformed ideas about sex. I wish I'd had that fierce actress who played Erin Brockovich's receptionist, the one who pretended to be a lawyer to scare those assholes from PG&E. She would've said something like "There are other medical problems that are often derived from a person's lifestyle, like lung cancer from smoking or diabetes from an unhealthy diet, but those aren't viewed with the same kind of vitriol and cold-heartedness." Then I would've smacked that doctor so hard in the face . . . No, wait. Violence is not our truth.

Scene 1, take 2.

Erin's receptionist would've grabbed me midstep as I leaned in to smack the doctor and screamed, "No, Jonathan!! You're better than this! We don't want you to get arrested! We just want your anal pap!"

Then I would've said, "Omg, you're right. Now, where's my butthole Q-tip?"

All of the ladies waiting behind us in the lobby would start to applaud and cheer. Aretha Franklin's "Respect" would come on the radio. Cut to us high-fiving with my anal pap results clutched in my other hand as we strut out to the car.

Sorry, I digress. Back to the safety net.

The largest population of HIV+ people in the US is made up of Black gay and bisexual men, but the largest population of *women* living with HIV is Black heterosexuals, like the ones Dr. Watkins-Hayes talks to for her research. Many spoke to her about their personal cognitive shifts that led them to seek help. "Some women will say something like . . . 'I just got sick and tired of being sick and tired,'" she told me. "Or 'I realized that I wanted to live for me.' . . . Because they had been doing things to please other people and they decided to put themselves first, or they recognized what it would mean if their families lost them.

So the cognitive shift is critical, but ... it's not just about waking up and saying, 'Oh, I'm gonna manage my HIV status.'"[5]

Nope. Next comes the real work. Scheduling doctor appointments, signing up for financial help, meeting with a psychologist if they want or need to. It's practically a full-time job, especially in the beginning and if someone's family and community aren't supporting them. Or if they have a job that doesn't allow breaks for doctor appointments, or if they live far away from a clinic and don't have a car or access to transportation. What if they don't have a computer or smartphone, or can't get someone to watch the kids? How is someone in these circumstances supposed to do any of this, especially if they live in a conservative state that hasn't bothered to work on its safety net? The communities at the highest risk already have so many hurdles set in place—a society rife with systemic racism and a political and economic framework designed to keep them down.

Luckily there are humans ready to help, not some random government voice from an 800 line who's just going to transfer you to someone else's voicemail. "With other safety nets, such as the welfare system for low-income mothers, your interaction with the bureaucracy is often organized around *not* getting you access to the services. There is an active push to discourage use of the system. But in the HIV safety net, it is the job of case managers to get you access to services so that you continue to stay connected to health care. That is what is so powerful about the HIV safety net relative to other safety nets. It sees connection to services as important for policy goals to be realized, and it uses the case management system to keep people connected," Dr. Watkins-Hayes said. "The HIV safety net creates a third-party intermediary to help navigate things on behalf of the client."[6]

As frustrating as that experience was for me, I was in a good place, even if it didn't feel like it in the moment. I was a white person who had a roof over my head, computer access, a car, no children to look after, and a job. So many of the 1.2 million people living with HIV/AIDS in the US don't have those same resources. (That number, by the way, is as of 2018. At the time of this writing, it's the most recent data available from the Centers for Disease Control and Prevention.[7])

In a state with strong Ryan White funding, an HIV safety net case worker is hopefully going to be a truly caring individual who will do everything they can to help a person out, and in ways far beyond simply booking appointments with a physician and a psychologist.

Look at Frankie Darling-Palacios, who's the outreach and enrollment coordinator at the Los Angeles LGBT Center. They've got around five hundred people on staff in five different buildings all across the county, but they still have to focus a lot of their efforts on education outreach because, as he explained, "People either don't know about us or don't want to come to the center." The patients they serve come from all over the globe—Egypt, Uganda, Central America, Syria, you name it—so there are cultural hurdles beyond the basic stigmas attached to HIV/AIDS that we have in the US. "We try to have as much cultural humility as possible when it comes to patient care," Frankie said. "I'm not the expert there—it's really about centering them. They're an expert in their experience, whereas I'm versed in the specific things they need help navigating."[8] He makes a point of sitting with each patient and helping them figure out a medical website portal instead of simply doing the work for them.

Another big part of LA's program is about community helping community, especially when it comes to trans health. "We hire trans people to help trans patients at our Trans Wellness Center," he explained. "They're not only trained in cultural humility but well versed in providing gender affirmative care at the facility. The rates of homelessness are higher for the trans community, and the rates of poverty are higher. The center is really the safety net in the community. They have clothing and makeup for women; they provide classes and employment opportunities."[9]

I was hardly the first or the last person to discover that California has a great HIV safety net in place. "Before the pandemic, you had a lot of people who took the first ticket from wherever they were coming from and came right to the LGBT Center,"

Frankie said. "It's still happening, even during the pandemic. If they're willing to take a ticket from wherever they are coming from, then it must be pretty hard."[10]

He's not wrong, but even in rural states with difficult health insurance issues, if you have a resource center working hard to uphold the HIV safety net, you can still find yourself in good hands. Say somebody like Amber Corey, who's the director of quality management and a case manager at the Heartland Health Resource Center in Sioux Falls, South Dakota. "Medicaid is hard to get here," she said. "Disability doesn't qualify you for it. You have to have been receiving disability for twenty-four months before you're eligible."[11] But because of that, her Ryan White funding can go a long way for those who need it because of its "payer of last resort" status. I've already detailed how stupidly expensive ART medications are if you don't have insurance, so for many of Amber's roughly five hundred HIV+ patients, it's cheaper to simply buy them health insurance using the funds.

"It's a really good deal as the economics of the program go," explained Lindsey Dawson, associate director of HIV policy at the Kaiser Family Foundation, a nonprofit dedicated to studying healthcare issues. "Even though Ryan White got a discount for purchasing HIV drugs, it was costly for the program to do this." The Ryan White program pays for individuals to receive HIV treatment services, and it's less expensive for the program to purchase insurance for people. So the individual can get other health issues, like diabetes or cardiovascular disease, covered as well.[12]

This is a great Band-Aid solution for HIV+ people, but what about all the South Dakota folks who *don't* have HIV and don't qualify for Medicaid and can't afford private insurance? They fall through the cracks, which is precisely why we should have Medicare for all. Since that doesn't seem likely any time soon, the best-case scenario we can hope for is that all states enact an expansion of the Affordable Care Act, since it introduced a lot of really important new coverage opportunities for people both with and at risk for HIV.

If you're HIV+ and live in a state that didn't choose to expand the ACA and you can't afford private insurance and don't qualify for Medicaid, you'd basically be up shit creek without a paddle if it weren't for Ryan White. And if your state chooses to not ask for much Ryan White funding, well, thank God for highways that lead to places like California—if you're even able to pack up your life and move, that is. Many aren't. It's not like any of it is easy, even in the places where it's easier.

That *Times* article I mentioned earlier, "America's Hidden H.I.V. Epidemic," centered largely on a Black man named Cedric Sturdevant and his work with an HIV social-services nonprofit in Jackson, Mississippi. I was curious how things have changed for him since 2017, and when we caught up over Zoom,

I learned he has since moved back to his home area of Greenville, Mississippi, to set up a nonprofit of his own. "It's in the Mississippi Delta, which is the largest rural area in Mississippi," he said, "and also considered the poorest area in the state, and somewhat the country as well."

He explained that he had decided to move back because, as a whole, the Delta area was comparable to Jackson in terms of people living with HIV, but with far fewer doctors and health providers. Transportation options are practically nonexistent. "The people getting into care really don't know too much about how to work the system, where to go, where they need to go. The stigma is very high here."

To help combat this, he co-founded and now serves as the executive director of his own HIV safety net, an organization called Community Health PIER. "It stands for prevention, intervention, education, and research," he said. "The thought is that when you go to a pier, . . . there's everything that you basically could want or need. That's the way we want to be as far as healthcare and health disparities, especially in minority communities.

"People in this area don't really talk about HIV," Cedric explained. "So what we're doing is basically trying to bring the attention back and trying to eliminate some of the stigma surrounding it. And LGBTQIA+ folks in general—there are no clubs, no bars, none of that for the community to really hang out. We have to mix and mingle with the heterosexual people, and most have to be careful of how they act. They can't truly be themselves."

The Delta area encompasses about twelve counties, but he says there are only around five healthcare providers spread around the area that treat HIV, and reaching one can be impossible for some. "As far as a bus system, that's not happening around here. It's very spaced out. You basically have to have a car to get around."

Those who can will travel to Jackson or even Memphis for their care, mostly because the HIV providers that do exist in the Delta all operate out of small towns where everyone knows everyone else's business. Cedric told me that PIER is working hard to combat shame, from both the community and the internal feelings of people living with HIV. "We want to empower them more to let them know they can still have a healthy life."

Cedric's staff is small, only three including himself, but in the weeks before we spoke, they'd managed to get twelve individuals living with HIV either back into care or to start care. For a staff that tiny and given all they're up against in terms of social hurdles, prejudice, and the challenges of doing outreach, that number is impressive.

Knowing how raw and vulnerable a time it can be, I especially appreciate how focused PIER is on getting involved as soon as someone is diagnosed. In some cases when a person is diagnosed via a local provider, the doctor or nurse will reach out to PIER before the individual leaves their office and give Cedric and his team a heads-up. This gives the nonprofit an opportunity to immediately offer support, which makes all the difference for someone newly diagnosed and terrified. "We want to make sure they know 'You can afford it. We'll get you in these programs. Here is what else you'll need.' We ask them if they need food or transportation. We try to make the load easier." Still, Mississippi is one of the states that didn't sign up for Medicare and Medicaid expansion coverage, and the only programs PIER has access to for help are Ryan White and the AIDS Drug Assistance Program. And while PIER can help people find housing, they can't access the available resources unless a patient has submitted an application from a case manager at a clinic, and there are any number of reasons why a person wouldn't even get a case manager, from fear of being seen at a clinic to the lack of transportation.

In terms of outreach and education, PIER has its work cut out for them. "We're focusing on stigma within the faith-based community," Cedric said. "We need them to stop the judgment and get educated. We're in the Bible Belt, and we need more churches and church members to be open-minded because it affects us all. Some of the really rural country churches still think that it's a gay man's disease."

Getting the right messaging in high schools is essential too since many of the newer cases Cedric sees skew younger, but that's an incredibly difficult task when the only types of sex education allowed are abstinence and something called abstinence plus, which means some schools will allow Cedric to talk about sex education, but with no images or useful presentations, like how to put on a condom using a banana as a prop—a more crucial demo than one might think.

"A lot of the guys don't know how to," Cedric said. "They think they do, but they don't know to check to make sure that the condom hasn't expired. They don't know the right way to put it on. Everybody wants to have an anaconda, but if they don't, they still want the Magnum condoms."[13] The obvious problem there being that if they're working with a garter snake, those rubbers are going to slide right off. (Serious, but funny.)

Cedric has devoted his life to helping people with HIV, and I'm sure you won't be surprised to learn that, similarly, the origins of the HIV safety net were built from the bottom up, not the top down. These systems don't exist because the government was trying to care for us. They exist because sick people stood up and demanded that their voices be heard, in activist movements like Gay Men's Health Crisis, first led by people whose numbers were rapidly vanishing while they fought because the AIDS epidemic continued to claim more and more of their lives in front of an indifferent country.

These grassroots efforts create a different environment and dynamic for people in need when it comes to the programs that developed because of them. There's less stigma because many of the people who built up the programs are either positive themselves or came from communities devastated by the disease. They understand what we need because they've lived it.

One of the wonderful things about the HIV safety net is that often after it has completed the initial work of saving a person's life, that person is sometimes so moved and changed by the experience that they end up becoming an AIDS activist, even if it's something they never imagined they'd do. "Part of what was so important about the HIV movement and continues to be important is the way in which marginalization and privilege work together within the movement to push the agenda forward," Dr. Watkins-Hayes told me.[14]

Even as a queer, nonbinary, HIV+ person, I know that in the context she's speaking of I land in the "privilege" camp, and part of what I mean when I say that being diagnosed with HIV saved my life is that it has also given me an opportunity to now help save other lives, to lift voices up and help guide people in need to critical resources. When I was growing up, I knew I wanted to help people, but I didn't think it would be helping people with HIV awareness and with my own recovery from various compulsive behaviors. But, hunty, sometimes that's how the cookie crumbles, and even if it's not the flavor of cookie I thought I wanted to eat, I still absolutely love all cookies.

CHAPTER 11

FIN . . . FOR NOW

Or, embracing my multi-hyphenate reality

I'm so grateful to still be on this stunningly beautiful yet imperfect road to becoming *America's Next Top* . . .

Oops!

What I meant to write is, I'm grateful to be on this stunningly beautiful yet imperfect road to becoming my most authentic gorgeous self.

When I think about my life so far, I'm both blown away and humbled by all the experiences I've had, the people I've met who've changed the way I see the world, and the lives I've been lucky enough to touch. When I was young I always thought that if I could prevent one kid from suffering the way I did, then my suffering would be worth it. I wanted to grow up and change the world, I wanted to make sure that kids like me wouldn't have such a hard time being themselves. I never knew what that could look like, though, or that it would look anything like what my life has actually become. I feel such gratitude that I've been able to bring joy and acceptance to so many people. I still struggle to comprehend that I could be someone else's Michelle Kwan.

If we're being honest, I did want to grow up to be famous, but I never saw a path towards being an entertainer. I didn't think it was a choice that was even possible for someone like me. As I got older, those childhood dreams faded into the back of my mind as the constraints and realizations of the "real world" started to set in. It took a baker's dozen years for me to come back to my earlier dreams. It took surviving sexual abuse, meth addiction, and an HIV diagnosis for me to start to listen to that little Jonathan inside me and take care of him, to reconnect with all of the goals he had for his future self.

The road I've embarked on since is one I try to make sure I don't take for granted. I know my trauma and my shortcomings will be right there along with me as I continue on my journey. I also know that much in the same way that I can't process something and then put it in a box never to be seen or heard from again, I can't fully understand the experiences of other people and attempt to put their experiences in a box either. Taking care of my inner child also means staying engaged and empathetic to people around me. There are so many ways that my early trauma still makes me have knee-jerk reactions to situations, where I'll immediately pass judgment on others around me as a means of protecting myself. I'm beginning to understand how these reactions can sometimes do more harm than good. (Though to be fair to myself, sometimes I am dead-on right, since a lot of these reactions are born out of survival instinct.)

For many people like me, as we grow it often feels like we need to rush to a point of security, or whatever the idea of security has meant to us. Whether it's finding love, owning a home, becoming financially independent, or never asking for help along the way. A part of me was always barreling towards a destination but not exactly enjoying the journey there. Being present in the process is a task I come back to daily, always knowing I could be doing better, especially since I realize daily how *not* present I can often be. Our society has taught us to act out of fear of scarcity, that if someone experiences success, their achievement reduces our own chances of achieving success. Our hopes and dreams can feel like they aren't destined for our reality. Call me Delusional Daisy, but I feel there is a world where there is enough for everyone if we can take care of ourselves enough to create space to celebrate one another.

I know that I put on a good show, but even with all the strides I've made, I still struggle with feeling worthy of my success and happiness. Referring to myself as famous still sends a chill of discomfort through my body. I feel pain in my heart when I think of all that I have when there are so many other people in the world facing endless struggles for basic human rights. I want everyone who is suffering to have the joy and happiness that I've found.

Acknowledging the shame I feel is my first step to feeling like a worthwhile person, because not acknowledging that allows me to disengage. The shame says I'm a bad person, the acknowledging says I can do better. Learning about what that guilt and shame say is important information for us in deciding what we let go and what we hold close.

The next step is understanding that I alone can't fix everything. I can do my best, but I can't do everything for everyone. Giving back can look different; for me it means being vulnerable with my voice and platform and communicating from my heart to make positive changes for the LGBTQIA+ community and humanity as a whole. It means being involved in giving to mutual aid organizations and supporting fantastic people doing important work, and it also means understanding what I don't know and staying open to learning and not getting defensive even when unsolicited advice gets hurled my way.

In my first book, I wondered whether you would still love me if you knew my whole story. That was so important to me at the time, but what I've learned since then is that I have to accept and have loving compassion for myself no matter what other people's opinions are.

The shame of my internal monologue says, *People won't take you seriously. You haven't earned your way into authorship or stand-up comedy success.* I know I have a valid perspective and opinion to share with the world, but that voice gets muffled by a fear of all the negative and outrageously hateful things I think people might (and often do) say in response. Even Evgenia Medvedeva, a two-time world champion figure skater, says she still felt like she needed to prove something to everyone. But then she realized she already had, that her skating was enough.[1] Thanks, Evgenia! You're saying I'm enough too!! Her words remind me of something that's often said in twelve-step recovery programs—that "fear" stands for "false evidence appearing real." I love that because it means I don't need to validate any of my actions to anyone, and you don't either.

I hope at this point in my life that I'm only approaching the end of my first act (even though it feels like I've already lived a thousand). For my next one, in addition to continuing to write, perform stand-up comedy, and create more art with hair, I want to expand prosperity to more people. I want to create a philanthropic foundation for LGBTQIA+ people and cats. Imagine a resource center that helps LGBTQIA+ people with applications for education grants, job training in fields as diverse as the people who come in, housing stabilization resources, healthcare resources, HIV and STI testing, drug and alcohol recovery resources, ice skating (obviously) and gymnastics and other sports training centers, a community garden, and an art center where everyone can learn to paint and sculpt and experiment with all other forms of visual art.

And all that is just at the west entrance!!

In the east wing it's all things cats and dogs: a center where anyone who is into animal care and rescue can help run the no-kill shelter and place the animals in loving homes.

Omg, is this a foundation or is it heaven?

Thankfully I found a husband who loves me and wants to help raise our five cats and two dogs while supporting all these dreams I have along the way. His support and joy for my heart and brain are sweet beyond any words I could write.

Creating a legacy of joy is important to me. Creating a world where we can learn that complexity is sexy and simply applying a categorizing judgment is most certainly not. Buddha said to live is to suffer. I believe that to be true, but to live is also to connect, to experience joy, love, wonder, and curiosity.

If you picked up this book hoping to find out how I stay so positive and how you can too, honey, I hate to tell you, but my Negative Nancy takes the wheel from my Positive Patty all too often, and having an optimistic outlook is a daily choice I have to make. The reality is that I'm still experiencing certain heartbreaks that I keep private. I'm not always the beacon of light and positivity I appear to be, the persona that gets amplified times a thousand since I'm on a TV show. I'm also disappointed, angry, irritated, and still dealing with trauma I've incurred throughout my life. In other words, I'm human. Life isn't about always feeling an unbridled positivity, but it is about nurturing the sad part while knowing that somewhere within you happiness does exist, and it's there to connect with when you need to.

Just as understanding how my past experiences affect my present, the experiences of others—not only in their own lives but in the generations that preceded theirs—requires me to constantly connect to empathy, patience, and ultimately a human curiosity that wants to help others find their joy and happiness. Above all the messages I try to share, this is the one I hope people will take most seriously. I don't have all the answers yet, but as I learn them, I'll be right back to share them with you.

I also need to just make, like, ten million dollars to build the JVN Heaven on Earth Center for LGBTQIA+ People and Cats and Dogs Too.

See you soon!

ACKNOWLEDGMENTS

So much gratitude to my family, my husband, Mark, who I love so much, and especially my mom, who helped me with research for this book, and to my dad, who I wouldn't be here without and who, however painful, let me write about our relationship. To the rest of my family, I love you deeply and wouldn't be who I am today without you. To Bug, Bug the 2nd, Larry, Liza, Matilda, Genevieve, Pablo, Elton, and Baggy, your love has healed me, and I love you all forever and ever. If you have a local shelter in your community, please support their work.

A huge special thank-you to everyone who gave their time and energy for this book, especially Joshua Lyon, Hilary Swanson, Rakesh Satyal, Fritha Saunders, everyone at Harper-One and Simon & Schuster UK, Aaron Short, Alok, Jason Lewton, Cedric Sturdevant, Celeste Watkins-Hayes, PhD, Ashlee Marie Preston, my therapist Marty, Marcia Vidal, Frankie

Darling-Palacios, Amber Corey, Lindsey Dawson, Carleen Orton, Karen Spring, John Spring, Owen Keehnen, Roy Birchard, Jeff Chen, Ryan Jude Tanner, and Jay Krottinger.

And my entire team who help me so much, for your hard work and patience, thank you for everything.

NOTES

CHAPTER 2: THE (CONTINUAL) EXPRESSION OF MY PERSONAL STYLE

1. Abigail Beall, "Why Clothes Are So Hard to Recycle," BBC, July 12, 2020, https://www.bbc.com/future/article/20200710-why-clothes-are -so-hard-to-recycle.
2. Institution of Mechanical Engineers, "35% of Microplastics Released into the World's Oceans Are from Synthetic Textiles," Phys.org, September 13, 2018, https://phys.org/news/2018-09-microplastics-world -oceans-synthetic-textiles.html.
3. James Conca, "Making Climate Change Fashionable—The Garment Industry Takes On Global Warming," *Forbes*, December 3, 2015, https:// www.forbes.com/sites/jamesconca/2015/12/03/making-climate -change-fashionable-the-garment-industry-takes-on-global-warming /?sh=51cff14779e4.

CHAPTER 3: QUINCY'S QUEER HISTORY

1. Jason Lewton, from an interview with the author, November 16, 2020.
2. Owen Keehnen, "Last Call at Irene's Cabaret," OwenKeehnen.com, last modified December 9, 2018, https://www.owenkeehnen.com /post/last-call-at-irene-s-cabaret-2017. Reprinted with permission. A longer version of this essay appears in *Sweeter Voices Still: An LGBTQ Anthology from Middle America*, edited by Ryan Schuessler and Kevin Whiteneir Jr. (Cleveland: Belt Publishing, 2021).

3. Lewton, interview, November 16, 2020.
4. Roy Birchard, from an interview with the author, November 17, 2020. Also see Roy Birchard, "What Do You Mean, 'I'm Not Being Spiritually Fed'?" *The Gay Christian*, First Quarter 1981, 9–11, https://issuu.com /mcchurches/docs/1980-4th-qtr-1st-qtr-1981-the-gay/11.
5. Chris Geidner, "Nancy Reagan Turned Down Rock Hudson's Plea for Help Nine Weeks Before He Died," *BuzzFeed News*, February 2, 2015, https://www.buzzfeednews.com/article/chrisgeidner/nancy-reagan -turned-down-rock-hudsons-plea-for-help-seven-we#.afza6xDEJ.
6. All comments in this chapter by Carleen Orton are from an interview with the author, November 12, 2020.
7. All comments in this chapter by Karen Spring are from an interview with the author, November 17, 2020.
8. All comments in this chapter by John Spring are from an interview with the author, April 28, 2021.
9. All comments in this chapter by Ryan Jude Tanner are from an interview with the author, April 29, 2021.

CHAPTER 5: THE DEVIL'S LETTUCE

1. D.A.R.E., "D.A.R.E.'s Position and Curricula Regarding Marijuana & Legalization," February 2, 2018, https://dare.org/d-a-r-e-s-position-and -curricula-regarding-marijuana-legalization/.
2. ProCon.org, "State Voting Laws & Policies for People with Felony Convictions," Britannica ProCon.org, last updated August 24, 2021, https://felonvoting.procon.org/state-felon-voting-laws.
3. Dan Baum, "Legalize It All: How to Win the War on Drugs," *Harper's Magazine*, April 2016, https://harpers.org/archive/2016/04/legalize-it -all/.
4. CDC, "Deaths and Years of Potential Life Lost from Excessive Alcohol Use—United States, 2011–2015," *Morbidity and Mortality Weekly Report* 69, no. 39 (October 2020): 1428–33, https://www.cdc.gov/mmwr /volumes/69/wr/mm6939a6.htm.
5. Nick Wing, "The Exhaustive List of Everyone Who's Died of a Marijuana Overdose," *HuffPost*, April 20, 2017, https://www.huffpost.com /entry/marijuana-lethal-dose_n_58f4ec07e4b0b9e9848d6297.

CHAPTER 6: A LOVE LETTER TO HAIRDRESSING

1. Don Miguel Ruiz, *The Four Agreements* (San Rafael, CA: Amber-Allen, 1997), https://www.miguelruiz.com/the-four-agreements.

CHAPTER 7: TERF WARS

1. Marni Sommer, Virginia Kamova, and Therese Mahon, "Opinion: Creating a More Equal Post-COVID-19 World for People Who Menstruate," Devex.com, May 28, 2020, https://www.devex.com/news/sponsored /opinion-creating-a-more-equal-post-covid-19-world-for-people-who -menstruate-97312.
2. J. K. Rowling (@jk_rowling), "'People who menstruate.' I'm sure . . . ," Twitter, June 6, 2020, 2:35 p.m., https://twitter.com/jk_rowling/status /1269382518362509313?s=20.
3. J. K. Rowling (@jk_rowling), "If sex isn't real . . . ," Twitter, June 6, 2020, 3:02 p.m., https://twitter.com/jk_rowling/status/1269389298664701952.
4. J. K. Rowling, "J.K. Rowling Writes About Her Reasons for Speaking Out on Sex and Gender Issues," JKRowling.com, June 10, 2020, https:// www.jkrowling.com/opinions/j-k-rowling-writes-about-her-reasons -for-speaking-out-on-sex-and-gender-issues/.
5. J. K. Rowling, "J.K. Rowling Writes About . . . ," https://www.jkrowling .com/opinions/j-k-rowling-writes-about-her-reasons-for-speaking-out -on-sex-and-gender-issues/.
6. Francis Galton, "Influence of Man upon Race," in *Inquiries into Human Faculty and Its Development*, 2nd ed. (London: J. M. Dent & Co., 1907; electronic representation, 2001), 200–1, https://pure.mpg.de /rest/items/item_2323042_3/component/file_2323043/content.
7. Alexandra Minna Stern, *Eugenic Nation: Faults and Frontiers of Better Breeding in Modern America* (Berkeley: Univ. of California Press, 2015), 155 and 167.
8. Soutik Biswas, "How Britain Tried to 'Erase' India's Third Gender," BBC News, May 31, 2019, https://www.bbc.com/news/world-asia-india -48442934; Jessica Hinchy, *Governing Gender and Sexuality in Colonial India: The Hijra, c. 1850–1900* (Cambridge: Cambridge Univ. Press, April 2019), 27–43. https://www.cambridge.org/core/books

/governing-gender-and-sexuality-in-colonial-india/hijra-panic
/1E3C6C60CC72BEDBBF1FD1559F83C505/core-reader.

9. Amit Katwala, "The Controversial Science Behind the Caster Semenya Verdict," *Wired*, January 5, 2019, https://www.wired.co.uk/article /caster-semenya-testosterone-ruling-gender-science-analysis.

10. Louis J. Elsas et al., "Gender Verification of Female Athletes," *Genetics in Medicine* 2, no. 4 (July/August 2000): 249–54, https://www.nature .com/articles/gim2000258.pdf?origin=ppub.

11. Anne Fausto-Sterling, *Sexing the Body: Gender Politics and the Construction of Sexuality* (New York: Basic Books, 2000), 111.

12. Abby Walch et al., "Proper Care of Transgender and Gender Diverse Persons in the Setting of Proposed Discrimination: A Policy Perspective," *The Journal of Clinical Endocrinology & Metabolism* 106, no. 2 (February 2021): 305–8, https://academic.oup.com/jcem/article/106 /2/305/6031005?login=true.

13. Jamie Wareham, "New Report Shows Where It's Illegal to be Transgender in 2020," Forbes.com, September 30, 2020, https://www .forbes.com/sites/jamiewareham/2020/09/30/this-is-where-its -illegal-to-be-transgender-in-2020/?sh=2cf06bf35748. See also: ILGA World, *Trans Legal Mapping Report 2020* (Geneva: ILGA World, 2020), https://ilga.org/downloads/ILGA_World_Annual_Report _2020.pdf.

14. Wyatt Ronan, "Breaking: 2021 Becomes Record Year for Anti-Transgender Legislation," news release, Human Rights Campaign, March 13, 2021, https://www.hrc.org/press-releases/breaking-2021 -becomes-record-year-for-anti-transgender-legislation.

15. Madison Hall and Canela López, "2020 Was the Deadliest Year on Record for the Transgender People in the US, Insider Database Shows. Experts Say It's Getting Worse," *Insider*, April 20, 2021, https://www .insider.com/insider-database-2020-deadliest-year-on-record-for -trans-people-2021-4.

16. Movement Advancement Project, "Equality Maps Snapshot: LGBTQ Equality by State," last modified July 23, 2021, https://www.lgbtmap .org/equality-maps.

CHAPTER 8: IMPOSTOR SYNDROME

1. "Margaret Cho–Notorious C.H.O." Cho Taussig Productions, filmed November 11, 2001, YouTube video, 1:36:15 (segment beginning at 8:49), posted by Venjix Pazuzu, June 3, 2020, https://www.youtube.com /watch?v=2EkMNnNnYFI.
2. Megan Dalla-Camina, "The Reality of Imposter Syndrome," *Psychology Today*, September 3, 2018, https://www.psychologytoday.com/us /blog/real-women/201809/the-reality-imposter-syndrome.
3. Samantha Simon, "25 Stars Who Suffer from Imposter Syndrome," InStyle.com, December 8, 2017, https://www.instyle.com/celebrity /stars-imposter-syndrome.
4. Mariah Carey, vocalist, "Make It Happen," by Mariah Carey, David Cole, and Robert Clivillés, Columbia Records, 1992.

CHAPTER 9: SORRY, KAREN

1. Dr. Elizabeth Rule, from an interview with the author, October 14, 2020.
2. "Why Are Domestic Workers' Rights Essential? with Alicia Garza," *Getting Curious with Jonathan Van Ness*, podcast, 51:14, October 20, 2020, https://www.jonathanvanness.com/gettingcurious/episode/1fb8c2e6 /why-are-domestic-workers-rights-essential-with-alicia-garza.
3. "What Happened to the Racist F***ing A**hole Dick Officials of the Confederacy After the Civil War? with Professor Robert Icenhauer-Ramirez," *Getting Curious with Jonathan Van Ness*, podcast, 1:04:47, March 31, 2020, https://www.jonathanvanness.com/gettingcurious /episode/26293047/what-happened-to-the-racist-fing-ahole-dick -officials-of-the-confederacy-after-the-civil-war-with-professor-robert -icenhauer-ramirez.
4. "What Happened to the Racist F***ing A**hole . . ." *Getting Curious*, https://www.jonathanvanness.com/gettingcurious/episode/26293047 /what-happened-to-the-racist-fing-ahole-dick-officials-of-the-confederacy -after-the-civil-war-with-professor-robert-icenhauer-ramirez.

5. CDC, "Racial and Ethnic Disparities Continue in Pregnancy-Related Deaths," news release, September 5, 2019, https://www.cdc.gov/media/releases/2019/p0905-racial-ethnic-disparities-pregnancy-deaths.html.

6. David Murphey and P. Mae Cooper, *Parents Behind Bars* (Bethesda, MD: Child Trends, October 2015), http://www.childtrends.org/wp-content/uploads/2015/10/2015-42ParentsBehindBars.pdf; and William J. Sabol, Thaddeus L. Johnson, and Alexander Caccavale, *Trends in Correctional Control by Race and Sex* (Washington, DC: Council on Criminal Justice, December 2019), https://cdn.ymaws.com/counciloncj.org/resource/collection/4683B90A-08CF-493F-89ED-A0D7C4BF7551/Trends_in_Correctional_Control_-_FINAL.pdf.

7. "What Does Pride Mean to You? with Ashlee Marie Preston," *Getting Curious with Jonathan Van Ness*, podcast, 46:36, June 29, 2021, https://podcasts.apple.com/us/podcast/what-does-pride-mean-to-you-with-ashlee-marie-preston/id1068563276?i=1000527317128.

CHAPTER 10: THE HIV SAFETY NET

1. "What Does Inequality Have to Do with HIV? with Dr. Celeste Watkins-Hayes," *Getting Curious with Jonathan Van Ness*, podcast, 1:08:23, December 31, 2019, https://www.jonathanvanness.com/gettingcurious/episode/29bb05b5/what-does-inequality-have-to-do-with-hiv-with-dr-celeste-watkins-hayes. Also see Celeste Watkins-Hayes, *Remaking a Life: How Women Living with HIV/AIDS Confront Inequality* (Berkeley: Univ. of California Press, 2019).

2. Dr. Celeste Watkins-Hayes, from an interview with the author, February 4, 2021.

3. Watkins-Hayes, interview, February 4, 2021.

4. Linda Villarosa, "America's Hidden H.I.V. Epidemic," *New York Times*, June 6, 2017, https://www.nytimes.com/2017/06/06/magazine/americas-hidden-hiv-epidemic.html.

5. "What Does Inequality Have to Do with HIV?" https://www.jonathanvanness.com/gettingcurious/episode/29bb05b5/what-does-inequality-have-to-do-with-hiv-with-dr-celeste-watkins-hayes.

6. Watkins-Hayes, interview, February 4, 2021.

7. Centers for Disease Control and Prevention, "HIV Basics: Basic Statistics," data as of 2018, last modified April 23, 2021, https://www.cdc.gov /hiv/basics/statistics.html.

8. Frankie Darling-Palacios, from an interview with the author, February 23, 2021.

9. Darling-Palacios, interview, February 23, 2021.

10. Darling-Palacios, interview, February 23, 2021.

11. Amber Corey, from an interview with the author, February 22, 2021.

12. Lindsey Dawson, from an interview with the author, February 1, 2021.

13. All comments in this chapter by Cedric Sturdevant from an interview with the author, April 26, 2021.

14. "What Does Inequality Have to Do with HIV?" https://www.jonathan vanness.com/gettingcurious/episode/29bb05b5/what-does-inequality -have-to-do-with-hiv-with-dr-celeste-watkins-hayes.

CHAPTER 11: *FIN* . . . FOR NOW

1. "Evgenia Medvedeva: Fans Have Saved My Life in Figure Skating Many, Many Times," FS Gossips, March 3, 2020, https://fs-gossips.com /evgenia-medvedeva-fans-have-saved-my-life-in-figure-skating-many -many-times/.